100% CONCENTRATED CHEATS, TIPS AND PASSWORDS!

Nintendo 64

A-Z OF CHEATS
VOLUME 2

Paragon Publishing Ltd
Paragon House
St Peter's Rd
Bournemouth
Dorset BH1 2JS
United Kingdom

Tel: +44 (0)1202 299900
Fax: +44 (0)1202 299955
Email: books@paragon.co.uk
Web: http://www.paragon.co.uk

A-Z of Nintendo 64 Secrets, Strategies, Solutions Vol 2
© 1998 RDT Ltd
© 1998 Paragon Publishing Ltd

British Library Cataloguing-in-Publication Data
A catalogue for this book is available from the British Library

ISBN 1-873650-70-1

All rights reserved. No part of this publication may be reproduced, stored in a retrieval system, or transmitted in any form whatsoever without the written consent of the publishers. This book may not be lent, resold, hired out or otherwise disposed of by way of trade in any form of binding or cover other than that in which it is published.

While every effort had been made to ensure that information contained in **A-Z of Nintendo 64 Secrets, Strategies, Solutions Vol 2** is accurate, Paragon Publishing Ltd makes no warranty, either expressed or implied, as to its quality, performance, merchantability or fitness for any purpose. It is the responsibility solely of the purchaser to determine the suitability of the book for whatever purpose. Due to the dynamic nature of leisure software, Paragon Publishing Ltd cannot guarantee that game cheats, hints & tips or playing solutions will work on all versions of a game.

A-Z of Nintendo Secrets, Strategies, Solutions Vol 2 is published by Paragon Publishing Ltd, an independent publishing company. This book is not published, authorised by, endorsed, or associated in any way with Nintendo, THE Games or any associate or affiliate company. This book is not and should not be confused with any publication that is printed or distributed by Nintendo, THE Games, or any associate of affiliate company. Nintendo®, Nintendo 64® and its characters are trademarks of Nintendo.

Thanks to: Andy McDermott, Nick Trent, Roy Kimber, Russell Murray, Lou Wells
Compiled by: Damian Butt

Published by: Paragon Publishing Ltd, Bournemouth

Other titles available in the Secrets, Strategies, Solutions series
For availability, or to order, call 01202 200200 (international dial +44 1202 200200), fax 01202 299955, point your browser to http://paragon.co.uk/specials or email books@paragon.co.uk

Lylat Wars Secrets, Strategies, Solutions • £9.95 • ISBN 1 873650 14 0
Super Mario 64 Secrets, Strategies, Solutions • £9.95 • ISBN 1 873650 07 8
Nintendo 64 Secrets, Strategies, Solutions Volume 1 • £14.95 • ISBN 1 873650 08 6
Tomb Raider II Secrets, Strategies, Solutions • £9.95 • ISBN 1 873650 13 2
Goldeneye Secrets, Strategies, Solutions • £9.95 • ISBN 873650 11 6
A-Z of PlayStation Secrets, Strategies, Solutions Volum 1 • £9.95 • ISBN 1 873650 19 1
Final Fantasy VII Secrets, Strategies, Solutions • £9.95 • ISBN 1 873650 12 4
For the best of the Net, check out What's Online at **http://whatsonline.co.uk**
A full list of available titles is on page 208 of this book!

100% CONCENTRATED CHEATS! NO WAFFLE, JUST TIPS!

Nintendo 64

A-Z OF CHEATS
VOLUME 2

CONTENTS

1080° Snowboarding	08
Aero Gauge	09
All-Star Baseball '99	10
Automobili Lamborghini	11
Baku Bomberman	11
Banjo-Kazooie	12
Bio FREAKS	57
Blast Corps	58
Bust-A-Move 2	58
Chameleon Twist	59
Chopper Attack	59
Clayfighter 63 1/3	60
Cruisin USA	60
Dark Rift	62
Diddy Kong Racing	63
Doom 64	65
Duke Nukem	69
Extreme G	70
F1 Pole Position	70
FIFA: Road to World Cup	71
Fighter's Destiny	72
Forsaken	73
Goldeneye mini guide	74
Hexen	124
ISS 64	126
J League Perfect Striker	126
John Madden	127
Killer Instinct Gold	127
Kobe Bryant in NBA Courtside	129
Lylat Wars	129
Mace: The Dark Age	131

Major League Baseball (Ken Griffey Jr)	133
Mike Piazza's Strike Zone	134
Mission Impossible mini guide	135
Mortal Kombat 4	151
Mortal Kombat Mythologies: Sub Zero	153
Mortal Kombat Trilogy	155
Multi Racing Championship	169
Mystical Ninja Starring Goemon	170
Nagano Olympic Hockey '98	170
NBA Hangtime	171
NBA In the Zone '98	172
NFL Quarterback Club 98	172
NHL Breakaway	173
Off-Road Challenge	174
Puyo Pujyo Sun 64	175
Quake 64	176
Quest 64	176
Rampage World Tour	177
Robotron	178
San Francisco Rush mini guide	179
Shadows of the Empire	192
Snowboard Kids	194
Tetrisphere	195
Top Gear Rally	196
Turok Dinosaur Hunter	198
Wave Race 64	199
War Gods	199
Wayne Gretsky's 3D hockey	200
Wayne Gretsky's 98	201
WCW Vs NWO: World Tour	202
Wetrix	203
World Cup '98	203
Yoshi's Story	203

1080° SNOWBOARDING

Transparent Boarder
Complete expert mode, then select Akari Hayami, hold C Left, and press A on his statistics screen.

Gold Boarder
Enable the transparent character and finish expert mode with him, then select Kensuke Kimachi, hold C Up, and press A on his statistics screen.

Panda
Come first in all time attack and trick attack modes. Select Rob, hold C Right, and press A on his statistics screen.

Deadly Fall
Select Match Race and finish all courses in expert mode.

Dragon Cave
Select Match Race and finish all courses in hard mode.

Penguin Snowboard
Perform all twenty-four tricks in training mode, then highlight the Tahoe 151 board on the snowboard selection screen, hold C Down, and press A. To perform all the tricks in Training Mode with ease, enter Training Mode with any character and perform some easy tricks, turning them red on the trick list. When you find a trick that's too difficult, select the trick list and choose an easy trick that you can do. Perform the easy trick and while you are still in the air tap C Right to switch back to the trick list. Then select the difficult trick and continue with the game. Land safely and the game will be fooled into thinking that you did the difficult trick!

AERO GAUGE

Turbo Start
Hold A and B while you're waiting at the start, then release B after the announcer says "Ready!" to get a much-needed turbo start.

Turbo
Ah, the world's least intuitive and player-friendly turbo function! If you need extra speed in the race, hold down A to accelerate, make a hard turn in either direction while holding Z, then release both buttons. If by some miracle you've got your timing right and haven't sent your car into a wall, you'll get a burst of extra speed. You can keep using the turbo until the temperature gauge rises too high.

Secret Cars and Tracks
To be honest we couldn't get this one to work, but maybe you'll have better luck. When the start screen appears, on controller two push and hold Up on the d-pad, then press R, L, Z and C Down simultaneously. You should now supposedly be able to play with extra vehicles on a new track.

Access F-15 And Mao-Mao
Wait until the 'Press Start' message pops up on the screen, then push C Left, C Down, C Right, C Up, C Left, C Right and C Down.

Play As Spanky
This is fairly straightforward, you just need to complete all the bonus missions and Spanky will be yours to command!

Play As Bad Guys In Deathmatch
For each level you complete in the normal game, you'll gain one enemy plane for use in deathmatch mode, up to a total of six.

Change Colours
Pressing R on the select aircraft screen in all the modes but deathmatch will give your plane a facelift. In deathmatch mode, you'll need to hold down R and select one of the four default aircraft.

ALL-STAR BASEBALL '99

2-D Players
On the main menu enter PRPPAPLYR.

Big Heads And Feet
On the main menu enter BIGHELIUM.

Big Heads, Feet And Bats
On the main menu enter GOTHELIUM.

Tiny Batter
Leave an open player lot for your team so it appears as 'Empty'. Select 'Home Run Derby', choose the 'Empty' slot and you'll get a player so small he is almost invisible. More time is needed for him to enter the batter's box before the pitcher can throw the ball.

Alien Stadium And Team
On the main menu enter ATEMYBUIK (a Thomas Dolby reference, no less) as a cheat code and the phrase "Let the abductions begin" will confirm correct code entry. The Alienapolis stadium now be available from the stadium selection screen and the Abductors team will be enabled for that stadium.

Nintendo 64 A-Z of Cheats Volume 2

AUTOMOBILI LAMBORGHINI

Mirror Tracks
To access the reversed tracks, finish the championship mode on both Novice and Expert difficulty.

Hidden cars
Bugatti EB110 – finish championship mode on Novice.
Ferrari F50 – finish championship mode on Expert.
Ferrari Testarosa – finish the Basic arcade mode on Novice.
Porsche 959 – finish the Basic arcade mode on Expert.
Vector – finish the Pro arcade mode on Novice.
Dodge Viper – finish the Pro arcade mode on Expert.

BAKU BOMBERMAN

Recover Quickly
Another feature of this quirky Japanese game that isn't immediately apparent is a way to avoid being stunned for long periods. Quickly rotate the analogue stick while you're seeing stars after being hit, and you'll be back on your feet a lot faster!

Secret Levels
On the very remote offchance that you've got a special Hudson controller, you can use it to access four secret battle levels. On the title screen, set the pad's Slow Switch to position Hu and wait until you hear a sound telling you the cheat has worked.

BANJO-KAZOOIE
Infinite Red Feathers
Enter Treasure Trove Cove and on the sandcastle floor enter: "CHEAT" followed by: "NOWYOUCANFLYHIGHINTHESKY". A cow will moo when you enter the letters of 'cheat', but you won't get any other indication that what you're doing is having an effect until you finish the whole code. Your red feathers total will not change, but you will now have an endless supply.

200 Eggs
To give Kazooie double the ammo, go to the word puzzle room in Treadure Trove Cove and spell out the word BLUEGGS.

99 Mumbo Tokens
Enter Treasure Trove Cove and on the sandcastle floor enter: "CHEAT" followed by: "DONTBEADUMBOGOSEEMUMBO". A cow will moo when you enter the letters of 'cheat', but you won't get any other indication that what you're doing is having an effect until you finish the whole code. Your Mumbo Tokens total will increase to 99.

20 Gold Feathers
Speak to the third spell book by activating the 321 switch above the pool leading to Click Clock Wood and then swimming to the stairs near Rusty Bucket Bay. You'll need to be quick as this is timed. When you've spoken to the book, go to back to the sandcastle in Treasure Trove Cove and enter "GOLDFEATHERS" on the sandcastle floor in the same way as you did the previous two codes.

Morphing Codes
The following seven codes are all accessed by playing the

Nintendo 64 A-Z of Cheats Volume 2

Bottles puzzle game. To get each code, you must first have obtained the previous one. To get the codes, go back to Banjo's house and once inside move so you're standing in front of the picture of Bottles that's hanging above the fireplace. Press C Up to go into look mode and move up to look at the picture, then press R to speak to Bottles. Complete the jigsaw puzzle within the time limit to get the first code. To get the other six codes, simply enter look mode and look up at the picture. When Bottles tells you that he has given you the last code, ignore him and look up again, as he was telling porkies, the crafty little fellow! When you've got all the codes (or as many as you feel you can handle) go to Treasure Trove Cove, find Rusty Bucket to lower the water level and enter the sandcastle. Enter the codes in the same way you entered the eggs and feathers ones.

BOTTLESBONUSONE	Big head Banjo
BOTTLESBONUSTWO	Big hands and feet Banjo
BOTTLESBONUSTHREE	Big Kazooie
BOTTLESBONUSFOUR	Beanpole Banjo
BOTTLESBONUSFIVE	Big hands and feet
BIGBOTTLESBONUS	Giant Banjo-Kazooie
WISHYWASHYBANJO	Washing machine Banjo

Level 1: Mumbo's Mountain

Jigsaw Piece 1

Start this level by running forwards and crossing the bridge to reach the other side of the water. Tread carefully when you reach the far side of the bridge as there is an unfriendly bull waiting to knock you down. You are unable to kill this bull with any of your attacks so make sure that you keep out of reach of his horns.

Now head to your right and climb the path up the side of the mountain until you reach the termite tower. Walk around the tower to the left and then follow the note path up another hill to the top. Search the area immediately to your left and you will discover a molehill and your first new trick for this level. Once you have learned this new technique you can collect your first Jigsaw piece from the platform in the centre of this area.

Jigsaw Piece 2
When you have picked up your first puzzle piece, make your way back to the termite tower and use your Talon Trot to climb the slope on the far side. At the top of this little hill you will find a small group of huts surrounding the Juju pole. To the left of the huts near the cliff you will find another molehill. Walk up to the mound, press B and Bottles will explain your second new move. Once you have learnt this new trick use the Beak Buster to break open all the huts that surround the Juju pole. Each hut has different items inside which will spill out onto the ground when you bust them open. The first hut contains musical notes which you need to collect to open the note doors later on in the game.

The second hut contains blue eggs which Kazooie will learn to throw later on. There are no special items hiding inside the third hut, only an enemy that you will need to defeat. Break open the fourth hut and you can save the first Jinjo. There are five Jinjos hidden on each level and you will receive a jigsaw piece for saving them all. Inside the fifth hut you will find an extra life and there is a jigsaw piece waiting inside the final hut.

Jigsaw Piece 3
Before leaving the area around the totem pole take a good look at the shaman's skull in the corner. In the eye socket to the right is another jigsaw piece, which you can collect now or later. To collect this tricky Jiggy, stand underneath the eye socket and perform a Flip Flap jump which you learned in the training area.

Jigsaw Piece 4
Return to the termite tower in the centre and walk back down the path to the bull pit. Once at the bottom, turn to the right and walk towards the huge ape who's stood on top of the tree in the centre. As you approach the tree, Conga will begin to throw oranges at you from his high up perch, which you must avoid. Around the tree

on the floor you will notice three squares marked with oranges. When all three of these squares are stained with orange juice you will win a jiggy piece from Conga. To stain the squares you must stand on top of them in turn and then wait for Conga to throw an orange at you. As soon as he has unleashed his fruity bomb, dash out of the way and the orange should crash down on top of the square. Once all three squares have been stained with juice Conga will reward you with a puzzle piece.

Jigsaw Piece 5

Behind Conga's tree in the corner is a small chimp who is complaining about being hungry. Chimpy likes oranges and you will need to find one for him if you wish to find the next Jigsaw piece. Dash back to Conga's tree; avoiding the everlasting barrage of oranges he will hurl at you, and jump onto the trunk. Climb the tree and near the top you can pick up an orange which you can give to Chimpy. Chimpy is very pleased with the food you have brought for him and rewards you with a Jigsaw piece before he runs away. As Chimpy leaves, the block of wood that he was standing on will rise up from the ground with your puzzle piece on the top. Jump onto this platform and collect the fifth Jiggy, then perform a Flip Flap jump up onto the higher platform around the edge. In the corner to your left is another molehill and your last new trick for you to learn on this level.

Jigsaw Piece 6

Once you have learnt your last trick for this level you can start practising this new technique, by firing eggs at Conga. Move to the platform nearest his tree and take aim. As soon as you hit Conga with an egg he will begin to throw oranges at you, so be prepared to retreat a few paces before moving in to open fire again. Once you have successfully hit Conga several times he will admit defeat and reward you with another Jigsaw piece.

Jigsaw Piece 7

Now that you have practised your new shooting move, it's time to find another target to blast at. Return to the termite tower and

b proceed up the hill to the right, heading towards the now demolished huts. In the centre of the crushed ring of huts is the Juju pole which will ask to be fed with blue stones as you approach it. Crouch down, take aim, and then fire eggs into the totem pole's mouth as it rotates in front of you. Every time you score a direct hit, a piece of the totem pole will disappear, but as it does so the remaining heads will rotate faster. Shoot three of the heads away, then stop before shooting the last remaining head.

High above the totem pole is a very special honeycomb piece which you will be unable to reach without the help of the last head of the totem pole. Jump onto the last head and grab the honeycomb piece. Now take aim and fire an egg into the final head. This head is rotating at a great speed so you will need to fire before you can actually see the open mouth. Feed this final head with an egg and you will be rewarded with another jigsaw piece.

Jigsaw Piece 8

To find the eighth puzzle piece you will need to use your Talon Trot to search the steep slope heading down towards the start point. Press and hold the Z button, then press C-Left and Banjo will hop onto Kazooie's back. Now slowly walk down the steep slope and you will find 18 musical notes and the eighth jigsaw piece on small platforms cut into the slope. Whilst running around on the slopes keep the R button held to fix the camera behind your back. This will help you to see where you are going as the slope will obstruct your normal camera position.

Jigsaw Piece 9 (5 Jinjos)

To find the last puzzle piece for this level you must find all five Jinjos imprisoned by the witch. We have already uncovered the first of the hidden Jinjos, found hiding in the fourth hut when we earned jigsaw piece 2. To find the other four Jinjos, start by sliding down the steep slope towards the start point, and on a tall platform at the base of the steep slope. The second Jinjo is waiting to be rescued. Stand near the platform and perform a flip flap jump to get onto this tall platform.

The third Jinjo is standing on the island in the middle of the small pond. Run onto the bridge, then turn to your right and jump and flap to reach this tiny island. Once you have rescued this little blue Jinjo, jump back to the bridge and continue into the bull's arena. Dodge the charging bull and then use your Talon Trot to search the steep slope to your right. There are several platforms cut into the steep slope, and the fourth Jinjo can be found on the platform in the centre.

Now Talon Trot up the hill to the monument at the top and then climb the slanted slab to your right. Once on top of the monument, follow the circular platform; collecting 14 musical notes on the way to the final Jinjo located on the far corner. As soon as you reach the last Jinjo you will be rewarded with the ninth Jigsaw piece.

Jigsaw Piece 10

In your new termite form (see Mumbo Tokens) you will have no difficulty in climbing the slanted platforms that climb up inside the tower. Jump from platform to platform in a circular formation until you reach the first floor where you will find a termite protecting six musical notes. Grab these goodies and then continue to climb up the circular platforms until you reach the second floor. There is another termite waiting here and a few eggs for you to collect if you are in short supply. Now you are ready proceed to climb the platforms to the top of the tower. Exit the tower through the door in the side and grab the extra life to your right, then follow the spiral slope around to the very top of the tower. Right at the very top of the termites's tower you will find the tenth and final jigsaw piece.

Mumbo Mountain Secret Switch

Use Chimpy's platform to leap up onto the upper ledge, then jump across the platforms on the left hand side. On the final platform is the first witch switch, that releases a Jigsaw piece inside Gruntilda's lair. This jiggy will appear outside the level, on the top of Mumbo's Mountain and can only be collected when you are in termite form.

Level 2: Treasure Trove Cove

Jigsaw Piece 1

From the start head for shore and follow the path directly ahead. Beyond the wall you will find a large rock pool and the remains of a ship that is stranded on the shore. Walk around the ship and use the crate to climb aboard, then speak with Cap'n Blubber who is strolling around on deck. The miserable Cap'n has lost his gold and hints that you may be rewarded for finding it. Jump into the large rock pool beside the ship and swim through the hole in the side.

A thorough search of the sunken hold will reveal the first half of the Captain's lost treasure. To find the remaining treasure, swim back through the hole and return to the ship's deck, then use your Beak Buster move to open the other half of the hold. Dive into the water and search the bottom of the hold and you will recover the other half of the captain's lost treasure. Now jump back onto the crate and perform a Flip Flap jump to return to the main deck of the ship. Return the gold to Cap'n Blubber and he will reward you with your first Treasure Trove Cove Jiggy.

Jigsaw Piece 2

After returning the captain's treasure, jump down from the ship and climb the crates to the left of the large rock pool. On the platform at the top you will find a Molehill, where Bottles is waiting to teach you a new move. Once you have learned the new spring jump technique, walk along the walkway and use the shock jump discs to jump from platform to platform moving to your left. Finally, leap over to the platform on the side of the large rock face and spring up to the platform at the top. Inside a little nook at the top of this set of platforms is the second Jigsaw piece.

Jigsaw Piece 3

Drop carefully down from the high platform and return to Cap'n Blubber's ship. Climb the crates again to return to the point where you learnt your new jump and then look over the edge towards the shore line. On a small platform you will find a bucket that has a hole in it, and it needs to be plugged with something.

Nintendo 64 A-Z of Cheats Volume 2

Drop down to stand next to the bucket and fire eggs into the top. Firing eggs forward has not got the right trajectory to fill the hole so you will need to launch the eggs from behind. When you have plugged the hole the bucket will empty the water from the little pool below you, and you can jump down to enter the sand castle. Once inside the sand castle there is a little game for you to play, where you must spell out the names of our two budding adventurers. You must use your Beak Buster move to stomp the two starting arrows, and then the letters spelling "BANJO KAZOOIE." You must stomp each letter in order, and then once all the letters have been activated, the gate at the far end of the sand castle will open and you can collect the next Jigsaw piece.

Jigsaw Piece 4
Exit the sand castle and head back towards the start point. Continue along the path and you will find yourself on Nipper's beach with a large hermit crab guarding the shore line. As you approach Nipper he will issue a warning and then will begin to attack you. To fight with Nipper you must dash in after he has attacked with his pinchers and use your Rat-A-Tat attack to peck him in the eye. After you have successfully pecked him three times he will admit defeat and disappear; leaving you to explore his empty shell. Run along the watery passage grabbing the musical notes and then use your Beak Buster move to destroy the two smaller crabs waiting in the room at the centre. With the crabs out of your way you can grab the next Jigsaw piece dangling in the sunlight.

Jigsaw Piece 5
Exit the shell and return to Cap'n Blubber's ship, and use your Talon Trot move to climb the rigging to the top. Bottles is waiting here to teach you how to make Kazooie fly using the special flying discs. After you have learnt your second lesson for this level, stand on the flying disc and take off. Fly directly into the cove and locate the two crevices on either side as you fly through. Land beside the box in the crevice to the left and then perform a Flip Flap jump to leap into the chest. Inside this treasure chest you will find the fifth Jigsaw piece.

Jigsaw Piece 6

Jump down into the water below and quickly return to the shore near Cap'n Blubber's boat. Follow the path to the left and continue past the shock disc platforms, then walk onto the wooden bridge to approach the spiral tower in the bay. Jump from platform to platform up the spiral tower and climb to the very top where you will find a large red X and a flying disc.

Use your Beak Buster move to stomp on the large red X and it will change into an arrow pointing in the direction of the next red X. Stand on the flying disc and launch yourself into the air and follow the arrow to the next place where X marks the spot. Land carefully next to the next X and stomp on the ground to make the next arrow appear, then use the flying disc again to take off in search of the next red X.

Once you have found all five of these symbols and stomped them, the last X will turn into a giant question mark. Look over the edge of the platform and you will notice the final X on a small island in the bay. Jump off the tall platform you are standing on and leap towards this small island. Kill the waiting crab and then stomp on the final X to make the treasure chest appear, then use your Rat-A-Tat attack to prise open the box. Inside you will find the next Jigsaw piece.

Jigsaw Piece 7

Leave the island, return to the shore and then turn to the right and return to the shore side near the spiral tower. Jump into the water and swim to the first floating crate, and then wait for the shark to retreat. When Snacker has moved, jump back into the water and swim towards the next crate to your left and then jump onto the platform again to your left. There are some wooden stairs here, but ignore them and follow the thin ledge that leads off behind the steps. Jump onto the three crates around the corner and then leap onto the larger platform to your left. Keep following the line of platforms around the edge, and you will discover the seventh Jigsaw piece in a small niche at the end.

Jigsaw Piece 8
Follow the line of platforms back to the foot of the wooden stairs and use your Talon Trot move to climb up to the next floor. Now climb a further set of wooden steps up to the next floor and search the chest for some Mumbo Tokens. Now climb the final staircase and then dive into the rock pool at the top. Dodge the mine floating around in the centre of the rock pool and swim down to collect the next Jiggy from the bottom.

Jigsaw Piece 9 (5 Jinjos)
Exit the pool and drop down to the platform below, then run around the outer lip and you will find the first Jinjo waiting on the tip. Drop down the line of platforms then walk across the wooden bridge to the right and find a flying disc. Launch yourself into the air and fly back to Cap'n Blubbers ship, then climb the mast to the top where you will find another Jinjo.

Rescue this stranded Jinjo, then return to the start point and leap over the edge into the water below. Underneath the start platform you will find the next Jinjo, but you must swim fast to avoid being eaten by Snacker the Shark! Swim quickly back to shore and then return to the area where you learnt your new spring jump move. Jump across from platform to platform, this time heading to the right. On the last shock jump disc you will find the fourth Jinjo to rescue.

To find the final Jinjo, return to the top of Cap'n Blubber's boat and use the flying disc to take off. Fly into the cove and enter the little niche on the right hand side. Climb the stairs to the top and you will find yourself at the foot of a big spiral hill. Turn to your left and walk around the edge of the hill and you will notice the final Jinjo on top of a tree to your left. Leap onto this tree and save the last Jinjo and you will receive the ninth Jigsaw piece.

Jigsaw Piece 10
Jump back across to the large grassy area in the centre of the island, and climb the spiral slope to the lighthouse at the top. Stop in front of the door and use the Beaky Barge move to break into the lighthouse. Grab the line of notes at the top of the lighthouse,

b) then use the special shock jump disc to launch yourself up to the very top of the lighthouse. Sitting right on top of the lighthouse you will find the tenth and final Jiggy for this level.

Treasure Trove Cove Secret Switch

Behind the lighthouse at the top of the island, there is a secret witch switch. This switch will release the third jiggy in Gruntilda's lair, by shooting it from the cannon just outside the entrance to the level. When you leave this level be sure to remember to climb the side of the ship in the entrance area to grab this special Jiggy.

Level 3: Clanker's Cavern

Jigsaw Piece 1

From the start, jump down from the pipe and run forwards towards the large pool at the far end. Dive into the water and swim around to the far wall and then swim through the underwater tunnel into the large pool beyond. As you approach the end of the tunnel Clanker will stop you and ask you for some air. This will be your first task, but it is a long swim and you will need to surface to fill up on air.

After grabbing a healthy handful of fresh air, dive down to the bottom of the pool and locate the hole in the middle of the floor. Follow Clanker's chain down to the very bottom and then find Gloop, a friendly fish that blows large air bubbles for you to collect. Swim after Gloop and fill up your air meter, by swimming into the air bubbles that float away behind him. Now it is time to turn the key that will loosen the chain holding Clanker under the water. Swim through the key and it will begin to turn, then find Gloop again to keep your air metre filled up. Turn this key three times and the chain will have loosened enough to allow Clanker to breathe fresh air again. Clanker will reward you with a Jiggy but you will need to return to the surface to collect it, so find Gloop again and top up your air levels.

You will not want to return here later in the game, so grab the eight musical notes around the bottom and rescue the first Jinjo waiting around the other side of the key block. When you are ready, return to the surface of the pool and jump onto Clanker's back where you will find the first Jigsaw piece on this level.

Nintendo 64 A-Z of Cheats Volume 2

Jigsaw Piece 2
As soon as you have collected the first jigsaw piece, Clanker will start to moan about having toothache from eating too much garbage. To solve his little problem you must knock out a rotting tooth from either side of his mouth. Jump back into the water and swim around to face Clanker, then stand on one of the platforms on either side of his head. Take aim at the gold coloured tooth and fire eggs until the rotten tooth falls out. Repeat the process for both teeth, and then Clanker will thank you but unfortunately he has swallowed your reward. Dive into the water and swim through the hole in Clanker's teeth. On one side of Clanker's mouth you will find a mumbo token and on the other you can find the next jigsaw piece.

Jigsaw Piece 3
From your platform, drop down inside Clanker's mouth and fight the three crabs running around the sides of the pool. Now dive into the water and swim through the passage – avoiding the moving tentacles – and surface in the large pool beyond. Move to the right hand side and jump onto the crate floating in the water, then take a good look at your surroundings.

You must swim or jump through the hoops in the correct order in order to win the next Jigsaw piece. Start by jumping through the green hoop in front of you and then head to the left to swim through the next green hoop. As you swim through the hoops they will disappear and the next hoop will change colour from blue to green. Swim or jump through all the hoops in the correct order and within your 50 second time limit, and you will be awarded with the next jigsaw piece. If you fail, all the hoops will return and you will have to start the obstacle course again.

Jigsaw Piece 4
Exit Clanker's stomach by swimming through one of the tunnels on either side and you will return to the large pool outside. Hop onto Clanker's back and run up to the tip of his tail where you will notice a Jiggy hidden behind a metal grill. Stand on the tip of Clanker's tail and shoot the metal gate with your eggs. Once you

have hit the gate several times, it will rise and open and allow you to collect this next Jigsaw piece. Jump from the tail onto the small round platform in front of you, and then drop onto the thin pipe behind. From here you can perform a Flip Flap jump to get into the nook to collect the fourth jigsaw piece.

Jigsaw Piece 5
From your platform, dive into the water to your right, and locate an underwater passage. Swim through this tunnel and you will arrive in the small cave where the Snippet Mutants wait. As soon as you enter this cave the Snippet Mutants will issue their challenge and start to attack. Jump into the air and use your Beak Buster attack to crush their shells and defeat these nasty mutants quickly. When all four Snippet Mutants have been killed you can edge around the side of their small rock pool and perform a Flip Flap jump to get up onto the thin ledge. Now walk towards the centre and leap onto the central platform to collect the next Jigsaw piece.

Jigsaw Piece 6
Swim back to the main pool area and then surface to grab a breath of fresh air. Now dive back under the water and search the underwater passage just to the left of the tunnel you just explored. Swim as quickly as you can through this tunnel and you will find the sixth jigsaw piece at the very end of the passage. Unfortunately, the way out here is blocked, so you will need to return the way you came in order to avoid drowning. As soon as you have picked up this tough puzzle piece, swim back the way you came and return to the surface of the pool.

Jigsaw Piece 7
Jump onto Clanker's back and move towards his head. Stand on the small round platform inside Clanker's blowhole and wait to be launched up to the platform above. Quickly jump off the small disc at the top and then carefully edge along the thin ledge towards the next puzzle piece. Stand underneath the small niche and perform a Flip Flap jump to grab the seventh Jiggy.

Nintendo 64 A-Z of Cheats Volume 2

Jigsaw Piece 8
Dive into the water from your high up platform and then climb back onto Clanker's back. Approach the blowhole at the front of Clanker's body then drop down into the blowhole when the small disc is fired upwards. Once inside carefully walk forwards away from the witch switch and dodge all the spinning blades. At the far end of this treacherous passage you will find the eighth jigsaw piece.

Jigsaw Piece 9
Continue to walk through the passage and you will fall onto a flying disc above the stomach pool. Launch yourself into the air and fly across the stomach area and into the passage in the far wall. Once inside the passage on the other side you will notice more spinning blades, only this time they are rotating a lot faster. Stop before the spinning blades and speak with Bottles who will appear from the molehill to your left. Once Bottles has taught you your new move, use this special invincible move to run to the far end of the passage. With your shield to protect you, you can reach the ninth jiggy at the end of the passage without sustaining any damage. But you will need to keep a supply of yellow feathers in order to return back the way you came.

Jigsaw Piece 10
Jump down into the large pool in the stomach area and swim to the exit tunnel to your left. You have already collected the first Jinjo from the bottom of the pool where you turned the key, so now to collect the second.

Run past the bee hive in the surface height exit tunnel and then dive into the small pool behind. Swim down to the bottom of the pool and you will find the second Jinjo that has been imprisoned on this level. Exit Clanker's stomach and swim into the underwater passage opposite the blocked tunnel where you collected the sixth Jiggy. In the middle of this passage you will find the third Jinjo on this level.

Now exit this passage and swim to the opposite side of the pool, where you will see an extra life on top of a platform. Stand on

Clanker's fins to jump onto this platform and then use the shock jump disc to leap up to your left. Climb the pole to the top, and then leap across to the left again and you will land on a high up platform. Use your Beak Buster move to smash the grate beneath your feet, and rescue the fourth Jinjo from inside. Now swim back to the start area and climb the ladder on the right to reach the platforms around the edge. Move around the ledge and you will find the final Jinjo behind the bee hive on the central platform.

Clanker's Cavern Secret Switch

Inside Clanker's blowhole you will find a secret witch switch. Use your Beak Buster move to stomp on this switch and the two eyes on the witch portrait will pop up. Now exit the level and return to this area and stomp on both the risen eyes, and you will receive the next Witches Lair Jiggy.

Level 4: Bubblegloop Swamp

Jigsaw Piece 1

The first thing you will need in this swamp is a new move to help you to walk through the piranha infested water. Head to your left and you will find Bottles waiting in the corner. He will teach you how to use the wading boots. Once you have learnt this important lesson, grab a pair of boots and head out into the swamp. Stop on the platform with the jigsaw switch, and turn to the left and head for the next area of land. Now battle the two frogs and grab the next pair of wading boots from the corner, then run to the left again and stop beside the giant egg in the middle.

Use the shock jump disc behind the giantzegg to leap on top, and then perform a Flip Flap jump to grab the extra life floating above the egg. Use your Beak Buster move to stomp on the egg's weak spot, then drop down from the top and look for the next weak spot to bust open. Keep attacking the egg's weak spot and you will find the first Jigsaw piece on this level.

Nintendo 64 A-Z of Cheats Volume 2

Jigsaw Piece 2
Use the leaf ferry to return to the corner platform and then head back to the platform with the jigsaw switch. Jump over onto the leaf on the opposite side and then leap over to the next platform. As soon as you step foot on this platform the Flibbits – a gang of frogs – challenge you to beat them to win their Jiggy. There are two ways to beat these nasty bouncing frogs. The best way to defeat them is to stand in the centre of the platform and use your shield move to protect yourself while the frogs attack you. Alternatively, you can use your Beak Barge attack to charge them as they bounce towards you, although you will need to hit each Flibbit twice before they will drop dead. Once you have defeated the gang of frogs you will be rewarded with the next Swamp Jiggy.

Jigsaw Piece 3
After defeating the Flibbits, turn to the right and jump across to a small grass platform, then leap towards the large turtle directly ahead. As you approach Tanktup the friendly turtle he will complain about his feet which are feeling cold and sore. Jump onto each of his feet in turn and use your Beak Buster to relieve the pain. Once you have stomped on all four feet, Tanktup will reward you by spitting out the next Jigsaw piece for you to collect.

Jigsaw Piece 4
Enter Tanktup's mouth and approach the conductor standing at the front of the Tiptup choir. He will play his new song for you, so watch closely and then copy the song by Beak Busting the correct notes in order. There are three musical lessons for you to copy, each getting steadily more difficult to remember. Every time you fail to hit the correct note you will be penalised, so remember the conductor's lesson well. If you are having trouble remembering the notes, you can walk back to the conductor at any time and press B, then he will repeat the lesson for you. Once you have successfully played all three of the choirs favourite tunes you will be rewarded with the fourth Swamp Jiggy.

Jigsaw Piece 5
Jump back to the Flibbits platform and then turn to the right and jump

b across the grass platform and onto a shock jump disc. Use the disc to launch yourself up onto the tall platform ahead and then use your Beak Buster to break into the hut. Inside the hut you will find another shock jump disc, so launch yourself up to the next platform and break into the next hut.

Continue to jump up the platforms and break open all the huts to find a Jiggy waiting for you inside the final hut at the very top.

Jigsaw Piece 6
Jump back down from the tall platforms, and return to the central platform with the jigsaw switch. Now use your Beak Buster move to stomp on this switch, and the next Jiggy will appear on the platform above your head. You have a 45 second time limit to get to this golden Jiggy, so without delay use your Talon Trot move to run up the steep slope in front of you. Run around the ledge carefully leaving all the items that lie to the sides of the raised walkway. Move as quickly as you can along the walkway being careful not to fall off and grab the Swamp's next Jiggy from the platform at the end of the ledge. If you fail to reach the final platform before the timer runs out, just return to the jigsaw switch and stamp on it again.

Jigsaw Piece 7
Drop down from this platform and then return to the start area where you will see a golden crocodile. Feed Croctus with an egg and he will disappear, and the next croctus will appear. Now return to the jigsaw switch platform and Talon Trot up the steep slope, where you will find the next Croctus waiting to be fed.

Now drop back down to the jigsaw switch platform and head for the shock jump discs. Jump your way back to the top of these platforms and you will see the next hungry Croctus. Feed this golden Croc and then drop back down to the floor and head for the large Crocodile on the right.

Behind the large Crocodile you will find the next Croctus that you have to feed. Fire an egg into the Croc's open mouth and then run back to t he friendly Turtle. Behind Tanktup on the platform in the corner you will find the fifth and final Croctus. Take aim and fire an egg into the hungry fellow's mouth and you will be rewarded with the seventh Jigsaw Piece.

Nintendo 64 A-Z of Cheats Volume 2

Jigsaw Piece 8
Now return to the large Crocodile's head and follow the path to the left that leads up to the maze. Grab the wading boots at the entrance to the maze and then run through the twisting passages until you emerge on a ledge with another jigsaw switch. Use your Beak Buster move to activate this switch, then run along the thin ledge to grab the next Jiggy from the small platform at the far end. You only have a ten second time limit to reach this tricky jiggy, so without delay dash across the ledge and claim your prize. Once again, if you fail to grab the Jiggy within the time limit, return to the switch and activate it again.

Jigsaw Piece 9 (5 Jinjos)
Run back through the swamp maze and then jump down onto the platform behind the large Crocodile's head. Leap across the swamp and grab hold of the pole, then climb to the top before leaping across to the next pole. Jump from pole to pole until you arrive on the small platform in the corner. Climb the pole here and rescue the first Jinjo from the top.
Now drop back down and return across the swamp the way you just came, then return to the start point. You will find the second Jinjo on top of a small platform just to the left of the bridge. Once you have rescued the second Jinjo, make your way through the swamp maze and enter Mumbo's hut. Have Mumbo use his special magic on you, then walk through the small hole in the wall and return to the first jigsaw switch. Run up the steep slope and follow the walkway around and you will find the third Jinjo in the small alcove near the final platform.
 Now drop down from the walkway and head towards Tanktup the turtle. Run behind Tanktup and you will find the fourth Jinjo stood in the middle of the swamp waiting to be rescued.
 To find the last remaining Jinjo imprisoned on this level, head for the shock jump discs, and search around underneath these tall platforms. Rescue the Pink Jinjo from underneath the platform to the right and you will be rewarded with the ninth jigsaw piece.

Jigsaw Piece 10

Once you have rescued all the Jinjos, return to the large Crocodile's head and walk through one of the nostrils. Inside the Crocodile's head, Mr Vile is waiting to challenge you to an eating game. Walk up to the red crocodile and accept his challenge and Mr Vile will explain the rules. There are three games you must complete with Mr Vile, before you can win the final puzzle piece.

To win the first game you must eat more red yumblies than Mr Vile. To win the second game you must eat more red yumblies again, only this time you must take care not to eat a yellow yumblie by mistake. And to win the third and final game, you must only eat the yumblies that are pictured at the top of the screen.

The yumblies will change colour from red to yellow, so keep an eye on the top of the screen whilst you dash around eating as many yumblies as you can. When you have won this third game you will be rewarded with the tenth and final Swamp Jiggy. If you fail at Mr Vile's game he will chase and bite you, and you must compete in all three games again.

Bubbleqloop Swamp Secret Switch

On one of the tall shock disc platforms you will break open one of the huts, and find the secret witch switch hiding inside. Beak Buster the switch and the top of the witches hat outside the level will blow up. There is another Gruntilda's Lair jiggy inside this huge witch statue, and we will explain how to retrieve it later on.hen you are in termite form.

Level 5: Freezeezy Peaks

Jigsaw Piece 1

From the start, head to the left and use your Talon Trot move to run down the steep slope. At the bottom of the slope you will meet Boggy the Polar Bear, who is lying flat on his back, complaining of stomach ache. Leave the poor bear for the minute, and continue down the slope to the bottom.

Turn to your left and run past the fairy lights and head for the pile of presents to the left. Behind these presents you will find Bottles, who is waiting to teach you your new move for this level. Listen

Nintendo 64 A-Z of Cheats Volume 2

carefully while Bottles explains the Beak Bomb attack, then climb onto the stack of presents and launch yourself into the air using the flying disc.

Quickly fly up to quite a height to avoid the snowballs being thrown by several annoying snowmen.

Now it's time to try your new move, so circle around and fly directly towards one of the smaller snowmen's hats. When you are lined up perfectly, press the B button to launch Kazooie at the target. Scoring a direct hit will result in the snowman crumbling; leaving you a surprise in his place.

Fly around the entire level and destroy all of these irritating snowmen and you will win the first jigsaw piece. To collect this golden puzzle piece, fly up to the top of the giant snowman's hat and defeat the huge ice block.

Jigsaw Piece 2

Drop down from the top of the hat and land carefully on the rim. Now fall down through the hole in the rim to land on the snowman's nose. Here you will find the first of three presents that have been lost on this level. Grab the present and then carefully leap from the nose to land on the wooden platforms just below. Walk slowly along the snowman's pipe and you will find the second Jigsaw piece waiting inside the bowl.

Jigsaw Piece 3

Jump back out of the pipe and return to the snowman's nose where you will find another flying disc. Stand on the disc and launch yourself into the air and then fly down towards the snowman's stomach. There are three target shaped buttons on the snowman's chest which need to be activated, so circle around and use your new Beak Bomb attack to bust each button in turn. Once you have successfully activated all three buttons the third Puzzle piece will appear on the floor between the snowman's legs.

Jigsaw Piece 4

After grabbing the third puzzle piece, jump back to the main land and approach the box that is jumping around at the base of the large

Christmas Tree. Stamp on the box to open it and the Twinklies will pop out and ask for you to protect them from the Twinklie Munchers whilst they hop across to the tree. Stand between the twinklies and the first hole in the wooden bridge and then use your Rat-A-Tat move to knock down the Twinklie Munchers, as they emerge from the holes. Once you have hit one of the Munchers they will drop back into their holes for a few seconds before popping back up again.

Keep hitting these green munchers to enable ten Twinklies to reach the tree, then run around to the rear of the tree to find the light switch. Hit the switch with three of your eggs and then quickly make a dash for the flying disc near where you learned your Beak Bomb attack.

Fly back to the tree and then fly through the golden star at the top of the tree three times. As you pass through the star for the third time, the case containing the fourth Jiggy will disappear. Now land at the foot of the tree and jump onto the trunk in the centre. Climb all the way to the top of the tree and you can collect the fourth jiggy from the top of the pole.

Jigsaw Piece 5
Climb down from the top of the tree and take a look around the lower branches. On the lowest level inside the tree you will find the second present. You have already collected the first present from on top of the snowman's nose, so pick up the second present and then drop down from the tree. Walk back to the start of the wooden bridge, and then run around the edge of the chilly water to the opposite side of the giant snowman. On a small island here you will find the third and final present, so leap across the chilly water to grab this present. Now it's time to find someone who would like these three special gifts, so jump back to the main land and then return to the start point. Enter the igloo opposite the start square and give the presents to the three young polar bears inside. Once all three kids have received their presents, they will reward you with the fifth Jigsaw piece.

Jigsaw Piece 6
Exit the igloo and run back down the steep slope to the very bottom.

Nintendo 64 A-Z of Cheats Volume 2

Now turn to the right and run around the edge of the chilly water and then follow the thin path up to the start of the giant snowman's scarf. Run up the scarf to the top; grabbing all the notes and red feathers as you go, then stop beside the shock jump disc. Just in front of the shock jump disc is a small wooden sled, which is the fastest route down from this position. Jump onto the sled and ride down the hill and you will crash-land on top of the poor polar bear with a stomach ache. Boggy will thank you for finding his lost sled and will reward you with the next Jigsaw piece.

Jigsaw Piece 7
Run back down to the bottom of the slope and run around the edge of the chilly water to the right. On your right you will find Mumbo's Hut on a small island on the other side of a small pool of chilly water. Take a running jump across the freezing water and enter the Shaman's hut. Stand on the skull and press B to cast the spell. You will need to have collected at least 15 Mumbo tokens before you can operate this spell. Once you have transformed into your new Walrus form, hop across the freezing water and then jump into the large pool and swim to the far side. Jump out of the pool and climb the steep slope to your right and you will meet Wozza, another walrus who is waiting for a friend to give his Jiggy to. As soon as Wozza sees you in your new form he will give you the seventh Jiggy.

Jigsaw Piece 8
Now run back down the steep slope and return to the Christmas tree. Keep moving around the pool and you will find Boggy the large polar bear waiting to try out his sled. As soon as you approach Boggy he will ask you if you fancy a race, so hop onto the sled and the race will begin. Guide your sled through the red flags and beat Boggy to the finish line and you will win the next golden puzzle piece.

Jigsaw Piece 9 (5 Jinjos)
After winning the race, run back down the slope and return to Mumbo's hut, so you can transform back to your usual self. Now Jump onto the ledge that runs around Mumbo's hut and you can rescue the first Jinjo that has been imprisoned on this level.

Now exit the hut and grab the wading boots to protect your feet from the cold water and dash across the chilly pool to the three small huts. The second Jinjo can be found hiding behind one of these huts, so locate him before he freezes to death. Now return to the large pile of presents where you learnt your new Beak Bomb attack and search the roof. The third Jinjo is stood on top of the chimney stack near the flying disc. Rescue this Jinjo, then use the flying disc to launch yourself into the air, and fly up to the top of the giant snowman's broom.

Rescue the fourth Jinjo who is waiting in the centre of the broom and then jump over to the scarf around the snowman's neck. Run down the scarf to the bottom and then leap over to the platform where you met Wozza the walrus. Walk into Wozza's cave and you will find the last remaining Jinjo waiting on a small ledge to your left. As soon as you have rescued this Jinjo you will be rewarded with the ninth Jigsaw piece.

Jigsaw Piece 10
You will be unable to win the final Jiggy on this level until you have learnt the lesson on Level six. As soon as you have finished running around Gobi's Valley, return to the start of the sled race and use the Running Shoes to race around the course for a second time. If you manage to beat Boggy across the finish line you will win the tenth and final Jiggy for this level.

Freezeezy Peaks Secret Switch
When you have destroyed all the smaller snowmen you will discover the witch switch hidden underneath one of them. Stomp on this switch and the next Gruntilda's Lair Jiggy will appear on the top of the advent calendar.

Level 6: Gobi's Valley

Jigsaw Piece 1
From the start, run around the pool and use your Talon Trot move to dash up the steep slope. Jump onto the front paws of the large sphinx in front of you and then leap around to the platforms on either side.

Jump your way up onto Jinxy's back and you will find a flying disc. Use the disc to launch yourself into flight and then look to your left to find a small golden sphinx with a hoop above his head. Fly through the hoop and another golden sphinx will appear around the desert. Fly through all the hidden rings of the ancients as they appear and the first Gobi's Valley Jiggy will appear on top of Jinxy's back.

Jigsaw Piece 2
Grab the first jiggy, then jump back onto the flying disc and take off again. Now use your Beak Bomb attack to bash the target and then quickly land on the roof of the pyramid. Drop down into the door which has opened and walk inside before the time limit expires. Inside the pyramid you will find Rubee and he will help you to get your next Jigsaw piece. Before Rubee will help you, you must fire five eggs into the small basket which is rotating around the centre. Once the basket is full, Rubee will begin to play his pipe and the snake in the centre basket will rise up to the ceiling. Quickly dash forwards and climb up the snake's back and then stand on top of the basket lid at the top. Now perform a Flip Flap jump to grab the second Jiggy from above your head.

Jigsaw Piece 3
Exit the pyramid and use your Talon Trot move to run around the side of the pyramid. On a thin ledge behind the pyramid you will find Bottles waiting in his Molehill to teach you the last new move in the game. Speak to Bottles and learn how to use the running shoes, then follow the thin ledge around to the right where you will see a large square building.

Run around the rear of the building and then jump over the small pool behind. Continue to run up the steep slope in the corner and grab you first pair of running shoes. Quickly dash back down the slope and then run to the front of the large square building you just passed. When you run across the switch on the floor at the base of the tower, the door on the top of the roof will open for a short period of time. Continue to run as fast as you can up the spiral slopes and then drop into the hole in the roof. Once inside this temple dive down to the bottom of the pool and you will find the third jigsaw piece.

Jigsaw Piece 4
When you grab the temple Jiggy, the door at the front of the temple will open and all the water will drain into the pool below. Now exit the temple and run down the hill and jump into the pool at the bottom. Swim around to the left and jump onto the small platform in front of the steps. Turn to face the island in the centre and shoot three eggs into the mouth of the small golden statue. Once you have fed this little statue, the hidden pyramid on the centre platform will begin to grow. Swim to the right and find the next statue to feed and repeat the procedure again. The pyramid in the centre will grow a little more. Swim to the right again and feed the last statue with your eggs. Once all three statues have been fed, the pyramid in the centre will rise to its full height and the entrance becomes visible.

Run up the stairs and enter King Sandybutt's tomb, then you will have to face the maze. Run to the right and make your way through the twisting passages until you find the exit on the far side. Enter the burial chamber at the back of the tomb and you will find the next Jiggy inside the golden coffin.

Jigsaw Piece 5
Exit the tomb by the door in the burial chamber and then turn to the right and jump across the pool. Climb the stairs in front of you and use your Talon Trot move to run up to the top of the pyramid. Stomp on the sun switch at the top of the pyramid. Quickly dash down and run through the door before it closes. Inside this small pyramid, use your shield move to destroy the mummy and then grab all the goodies around the room. Now use your Beak Buster move to turn the floor tiles over and match the pairs. Once the floor pieces have been correctly matched you will be rewarded with the next golden puzzle piece.

Jigsaw Piece 6
Exit the room and follow the path around to the back of the pyramid, then head for the hot sand pool to your left. Jump onto the flying carpet when it passes by in front of you and hitch a ride

Nintendo 64 A-Z of Cheats Volume 2

to the island in the centre. Gobi the native camel has been tied to a rock in the middle of this pool and is desperate for some shade. Use your Beak Barge to break the rock keeping Gobi on the island, and he will reward you with the next Jiggy.

Jigsaw Piece 7
Jump back onto the flying carpet and travel back to the pyramid. Now follow the thin ledge back up to the corner and grab the running shoes. Dash around behind the large temple and then race to the corner opposite. As soon as you land on the corner platform, Grabba the Mummy's hand will appear; taunting you with the next Jigsaw piece. Dash forwards and leap at the hand and whisk the Jiggy away before the hand can close and disappear. You will never be quick enough to grab this tricky Jiggy without the aid of the special running shoes, so if the boots's magic runs out, return to the opposite corner and grab another pair.

Jigsaw Piece 8
Now return to the start area and swim to the small island in the centre of the pool. Gobi the camel is resting underneath the tree, but the tree is in desperate need of rain. Jump onto Gobi's back and then use your Beak Buster move to stomp on the camel's hump. As you do this Gobi will spurt water at the tree giving it the water it desperately needs. As Trunker grows back to full strength the next Jiggy will appear on top of the refreshed tree. Return to the large sphinx and use the flying disc to take off and grab this golden Jigsaw piece.

Jigsaw Piece 9
Return to the flying disc and launch yourself into the air again, and then land on one of the tall cacti in front of Jinxy's face. As you set foot onto the platform, Jinxy will tell you that his nose is blocked, so aim an egg into the nostril closest to you. Once you score a direct hit, Jinxy will tell you that it tickles, so jump over to the other cactus and fire an egg into the other nostril. Once both nostrils have been hit by eggs, Jinxy will sneeze and open the door

to get inside this final temple. Carefully drop down from the Cactus and enter the door, then perform a Flip Flap jump to leap onto the first magic carpet. Turn to face the statue on the wall and feed it with an egg and the carpet will rise up to the next level. Now turn to the left and jump across to the next carpet, and feed the next statue. As the carpet reaches the top of it's climb, dash to the left and leap onto the final carpet to grab the next golden jigsaw piece.

Jigsaw Piece 10 (5 Jinjos)
Jump carefully back across the carpets and then stop on the first carpet closest to the door. Feed the statue again, only this time turn to the right and leap across to the carpet above the door. Rescue the first Jinjo and then drop down to the floor and exit the temple. Turn to your left and run up the steep slope and then climb the stairs and enter King Sandybutt's tomb. Run through the maze to the burial chamber and you will find the second Jinjo hiding inside one of the three pots. Now exit the burial chamber and dive into the pool behind. At the bottom of the pool the third Jinjo is waiting for you to release him.

Now jump out of the pool and head for the sun pyramid in the corner, then use your Talon Trot to run around the sides of the pyramid. You will find the fourth Jinjo hiding in a little niche at the rear of the pyramid. Rescue this little fellow and then return to the start point. The fifth and final Jinjo is stood on the platform behind you, so leap across the hot sand pool and rescue this Jinjo and you will win the final Gobi's Valley Jiggy.

Gobi's Valley Secret Switch
Inside King Sandybutt's maze you will find a secret witch switch. Stomp on this switch and another Gruntilda's lair Jiggy will appear.

Level 7: Mad Monster Mansion

Jigsaw Piece 1
From the start, turn to the right and run around the large mansion in the centre. Around the rear of the house you will find another metal gate, use your Beak Barge move to knock down the gate, and then enter the churchyard. Around the churchyard you will find five small pots which you must fill with eggs. Fire three eggs into each pot and they will sprout flowers. Continue to fire eggs into all the empty pots and when all five pots are in bloom you will be rewarded with the first Jigsaw piece.

Jigsaw Piece 2
Now move around to the church entrance and use the tombstone on the right to jump up onto the church roof. Use your Talon Trot to move across the roof without falling and head for the clock tower to the left.

Hop onto the step and then follow the thin ledge around the clock face and then enter the small door. Now run around the edge to the front of the clock and use the shock jump disc to launch yourself up to the weather cock on top of the roof. Climb to the top of the pole and you can collect the second Jigsaw piece on this haunted level.

Jigsaw Piece 3
Drop down from the spire and head back through the churchyard gate and turn to the right. Drop down the small flight of steps and then use your Beak Barge attack to break into the cellar. Drop down into the cellar and use your Rat-A-Tat move to break open the barrels. In the last barrel on the left hand side you will find the third Mansion Jiggy.

Jigsaw Piece 4
Exit the cellar and climb back up the steps, then head across the garden towards the shed at the back. Use your Beak Barge move

to break open the door and then walk inside. Around the room you will see letters and pictures of Gruntilda and a glass tumbler in the centre of the room. Run forwards and jump on top of the tumbler and move it around the edges of the room. Spell "Banjo Kazooie" before the time runs out and you will win the next golden puzzle piece. Watch out for the nasty ghost who will try to knock you off the tumbler, and also avoid touching the Gruntilda squares as they will hurt you.

Jigsaw Piece 5
Leave the shed and then head to the left and follow a small path down to a gate. Turn to the left and climb the thin plank of wood and then drop down into the well at the top. Swim down to the bottom of the well and you will find the fifth Jiggy waiting in the bucket. Be careful while swimming around in this well as there are lots of tentacles trying to catch a piece of you.

Jigsaw Piece 6
Now climb the rope out of the well and walk back down the plank and then bust open the gate in front of you. Walk around the pool to the right and then climb the stairs in the far corner and you will find a pair of running shoes and a switch.

Stomp on the switch and the door to the church will open in the opposite corner of the level. Now quickly grab the running shoes and race to the church entrance, then dash through the door before the timer runs out. Walk along the aisle in the centre and approach the large organ at the front of the church. Use the steps to jump up onto the organ and then use your Talon Trot to climb up to the music stand where you will meet Motzhand the ghostly musician.

Motzhand will play you a song on his organ and you must follow along behind him and repeat the notes just after he has played them. If you can successfully follow both his haunting melodies you will win the next Jigsaw piece. To collect your golden prize, jump back to the music stand and then leap up to the top of the organ. You will find this golden Jiggy on top of the pipes.

Nintendo 64 A-Z of Cheats Volume 2

Jigsaw Piece 7
Exit the church and head back towards the large central mansion, then climb the drainpipe to get onto the roof. Use your Talon Trot move to run around the roof, then break open the two windows on either side of the building. Now use the shock jump disc to launch yourself onto the roof above and again use your Talon Trot to move around the sloped roof. Jump right up to the very top of the building and then drop down through the chimney. Walk out of the fireplace and then jump across to land on the chair. Leap from chair to chair and then jump onto the table and rescue the next Jiggy from underneath the sleeping ghost. Touching the floor in this room will wake up Napper, the Jiggy's guardian, so avoid falling off the chairs until you have picked up this puzzle piece.

Jigsaw Piece 8
Break open the door to leave this room and then head back to the churchyard, and jump over the wall to reach Mumbo's Hut. Walk into the hut, stand on the skull in the centre and press B, then Mumbo will weave his magic spell. Leave the hut in your new pumpkin form and then hop through the small hole in the wall. Now hop past the churchyard entrance and find another small hole in the left hand wall. Climb the slope and follow the thin ledge to the rooftop, and jump through the window that you opened earlier. Jump into the toilet and allow yourself to be flushed down the pan, and then follow the pipe to the bottom. In the corner you will find the next golden puzzle piece for you to collect, so grab the Jiggy and then hop back up the pipe to return to the toilet.

Jigsaw Piece 9
Now exit the window and hop along the tiles until you find the larger drainpipe at the front of the house. Drop down into this drainpipe to collect the ninth Jigsaw piece as you fall to the bottom. Now hop out of the hole in the bottom and return to the Shaman's Hut to return to your normal form.

Jigsaw Piece 10 (Jinjos)
To win the final Jiggy on this level you must find all five Jinjo's that have been imprisoned here. Return to the basement and you will find the first Jinjo hiding inside a barrel on the right hand side. Now run back to the churchyard and break open the gate that leads to the maze. Run around the maze and you will find the second Jinjo in the corner. Rescue this little fellow and then exit the maze and climb the drainpipe to get onto the roof.

Use your Talon Trot to dash across the tiles and rescue the third Jinjo from on top of the smaller chimney stack. Now head to the back of the house and leap to land on the window sill, use your Rat-A-Tat move to smash the window. Enter the room and then use the shock jump disc to leap up on top of the bed, and rescue the fourth Jinjo.

Now drop down from the rooftop and head to the side of the house with the small pool, where you activated the church door switch. Use the shock jump disc to leap over the tentacle and rescue the final Jinjo.

Mad Monster Mansion Secret Switch
Up on the rafters inside the church you will find another secret witch switch. Stomp on this special switch and the next Gruntilda's Lair Jiggy will appear in the eye socket of the large Witch's Head Statue.

Level 8: Bucket Bay

Jigsaw Piece 1
From the start, head to the left and feed the toll booth with two blue eggs. Now cross the bridge and use your Talon Trot to run up the sloped roof and down the other side. Jump onto the glass window and use the Beak Buster move to break the window, then drop inside the building. Now turn around and head along the plank and then turn to the right and jump up onto a crate. On the crate just to the right you will find the first Bay Jiggy.

Nintendo 64 A-Z of Cheats Volume 2

Jigsaw Piece 2
Jump down into the oily water and quickly swim through the open door. Now swim to your left and get out of the water using the ladder in the corner. Walk around the toxic pool and quickly run past the exploding box and use the shock jump disc to launch yourself up onto the edge of the first crane. Now perform a Flip Flap jump to get up to the crane controls, and then use your Beak Barge to activate the up button. Now quickly climb the ladder to your right and run across the top of the crane, then drop down to the ship's deck and grab the second golden Jiggy. If you flap your wings just before you land on the ship's deck you will not take any damage from the fall.

Jigsaw Piece 3
Now walk down the right hand side of the ship and climb a set of stairs to your left. At the top, leap up onto the platform above and walk round to the front where you will find three grey numbered switches. These switches play the ship's horns, so use your Beak Buster move to bash the switches in this order: 3, 1, 2, 1, 1, 1. Complete the tune correctly and you will be rewarded with the third golden puzzle piece.

Jigsaw Piece 4
Now walk around the back of the horn platform, and climb the ladder leading up the funnel. Climb to the top of the ladder then follow the ledge across to the other funnel and climb the next ladder to the top. Now walk around the ledge again and cross the bridge again to reach the first funnel. Climb the ladder to the top of the funnel and you will find the fourth Jiggy waiting for you in the centre.

Jigsaw Piece 5
Cimb back down and cross the bridge to the second funnel, and then walk down the ladder to the level below. Now leap off this platform and land on the huge stack of crates towards the rear of the boat. Leap from the highest crate and land on the TNT crate in the centre, then climb to the top of the rope and onto the crane.

b Walk across the top of the crane, and then head down the ladder to the operating switches.

This time use your Beak Barge to operate the down switch, and the TNT box will fall and break open the ship's hold. Now climb back to the top of the crane and drop down the hole into the hold. Inside the hold Boss Boom Box is waiting for a fight. You can use three kinds of attacks to beat this big box. You can use the Rat-A-Tat, Beak Barge or your invincibility shield to break through the wooden boxes. Each time you defeat a box, two smaller boxes will emerge from inside. When you have demolished all of the boxes you will win the next jigsaw piece.

Jigsaw Piece 6
Climb out of the hold and then head towards the front of the ship. Break open the small porthole window near the lifeboat. Drop down into the window and you will find yourself inside the Captain's quarters. Use your Rat-A-Tat attack to kill the sailors protecting this area and then use you Beak Barge to break open the cupboard door. Now jump into the cupboard and use your Rat-A-Tat attack to defeat the eel monster that will jump out from the hole at the back of the cupboard. Once this beast is defeated you can perform a Flip Flap jump to collect the next golden Jiggy.

Jigsaw Piece 7
Leave the Captain's room via the window and return to the rear of the boat. Drop down onto the platform at the very back of the boat, and then jump into the vent. At the bottom of the vent, use your Beak Buster to stomp on the fan switch and the fans in the engine room will slow down. Now leave this room and make your way to the nearest funnel, and break down the small door to get inside. Now climb the ladder down to the bottom and enter the engine room. Walk forwards and wait for the platform ahead to rotate. As soon as it stops moving, dash forwards and leap onto the platform on the other side. Now climb the cogs and then stand on the platform at the top and you will see a platform on either side of you. Wait until the shaft has stopped spinning and then dash to the platform on your left. Again jump across the revolving

Nintendo 64 A-Z of Cheats Volume 2

platform and you will find a switch. Turn to the right and jump through the fan when it slows down. Now turn to your left and the next Jiggy is waiting on the platform at the back of the engine room.

Jigsaw Piece 8
Head back to the switch you saw and use your Beak Buster move to activate it. As you stomp on this switch the propellers at the back of the ship will slow down, but not enough to let you grab the next Jiggy. Jump back through the fan and then leap past the fan on the far side and you will find another switch.

Use you Beak Buster again to activate this switch and the propellers at the back of the boat will stop spinning for a short period of time. Now carefully but quickly jump back across the revolving platforms and then climb the ladder to exit the funnel. Dash to the back of the boat and then dive into the water and quickly grab the next Jiggy from in between the two propellers. If you fail to reach this tricky Jiggy before the time limit expires, you will have to return to the engine room to activate the two switches again.

Jigsaw Piece 9
Quickly exit the water before you drown and then walk back to the two egg toll booth. Cross the bridge and then dive into the water near the front of the boat and you will see a dolphin that is trapped underneath the ship's anchor.

Quickly follow the anchor's chain up into the ship and then hop out of the filthy oily water and into a small passage. Kill all the eels will attack you along this corridor, and then drop into the room ahead and use your Beak Buster to operate the anchor switch. The anchor will now rise and the dolphin will be free, so return to the chain and swim back to where the dolphin was and pick up the ninth Jiggy from the bottom of the dock.

Jigsaw Piece 10 (5 Jinjos)
Jump out of the water near the start and cross the two egg toll bridge. Use your Talon Trot move to run across the slanted roof and then dive into the pool at the back. Now swim quickly to the corner to

avoid the hungry shark and rescue the first Jinjo from on top of the buoy.

Dive back into the pool and swim through the hole in the fence and then swim to the left and you will find another ladder. Climb the ladder and then hop from barrel to barrel across the toxic pool in the corner. On the barrel in the corner you will find the second Jinjo that has been imprisoned on this level.

Jump back across the barrels and then follow the ledge around the toxic pool and then head for the next toll booth. Feed the booth with four eggs and then cross the bridge and you will see three large containers. Use the crates at the end to jump up on top of these containers, and then drop down into the middle container from the top. Search around the crates at the bottom and you will find the third Jinjo waiting to be rescued.

Now exit the container and head back to the start and cross the gangplank to board the ship. Run to the rear of the boat and jump off the crates to grab hold of the rope from the crane and climb up to the top. Now drop down from the crane and feed the toll Booths on either side. Walk across the bridge from toll booth eight and carefully follow the ledge to the end. Right at the end of this ledge you will find the fourth Jinjo, so rescue the poor fellow and dive into the water.

Swim across the back of the boat and then use the crate to grab some fresh air before swimming into the small hole in the wall. At the bottom of the pool you will find the fifth and final Jinjo imprisoned in the Bay, so quickly rescue this guy and you will be rewarded with the last Jiggy.

Bucket Bay Secret Switch

Stand on top of the rightmost crane and leap across to the tall platform at the rear of the ship. This may seem like a long jump but it is possible if you jump and flap your wings in the air. Once on the tall platform, use your Beak Buster move to stomp on the witch switch and the next Gruntilda's Lair Jiggy will appear.

Level 9: Click Clock Wood

Jigsaw Piece 1
From the start, turn around and walk across the bridge and you will find the Spring switch on the floor. Activate this switch and the door to the first season will open, then walk through the door and enter the first area of this level.

Head over to the right hand side and jump into the water, then swim to the right and walk up the slope and follow the path around to the tree in the centre. Now head to the left and follow the path around the tree, then use your Talon Trot to run up the steep slope and continue to follow the path cut into the tree. Follow this path to the top and then you must leap around from platform to platform by jumping out and then back in towards the tree to land safely on the next platform.

Use the shock jump disc to launch yourself up to the next level and then continue to jump around the tree until you see a half built tree house. Stand near the front of the half built building and then drop down onto the platform below, now move carefully and jump onto the half built bridge. Walk along the wooden bridge; hopping the gaps until you arrive at Nabnut the Squirrel's house. Use your Beak Buster to stomp on the Summer switch. This opens the door to the summer season. Continue to jump from platform to platform climbing up the tree.

At the end of the next set of platforms turn to the left and walk around to the back of the eagle's nest and then use the shock jump disc to jump up on top of the egg. Use your Beak Buster move to break open the egg, and Eyrie the eagle will hatch. Leave the nest and continue to climb up the wooden platform around the tree. At the top of these platforms, turn to the right and use your Beak Barge to break open the door into the tree. Now enter the area at the very top of the tree, dodge the tentacles and grab the first Jiggy from the floor.

Jigsaw Piece 2
Exit the area at the top of the tree and then make your way back to the bottom of the tree, and jump across the thorns to Mumbo's

hut. Walk into the hut and stand on the skull in the floor and then press B and Mumbo will perform his last magic spell in the game.

In your new Bumblebee form, fly up to the very top of the tree and then circle around it and you will find the next golden puzzle piece on a small ledge at the very top. Fly through the snapping plant and grab this golden Jiggy, then fly back down to Mumbo's hut and have him change you back. Now jump back across the thorns and grab the wading boots, then dash for the slope to your right. Dodge the bull and jump over the small fence and fire three eggs into the hole in the centre. The plant will begin to grow. Now swim through the pool and exit this area and head for the Summer door and the next season of fun.

Jigsaw Piece 3

As you walk through the summer door Eyrie the eagle is awake and hungry, he will need five caterpillars to eat to grow big and strong. Run forwards towards the tree and the you will find the first caterpillar in front of the two leaves. Now head to the right and walk down towards the beaver's cave. Use your Beak Barge to break the rock in front of the beaver's house and then walk around the tree stump behind you to collect the second caterpillar.

Now continue to run around the lower area of the tree and you will find the Autumn switch in the corner. Kill the bird protecting this switch and then use your Beak Buster to activate this switch and open the door to the next season. Run back towards the beaver's cave and run up the slope in the left hand corner and head towards the large tree in the centre. Dash to the right and then follow the next path back down to the flower where you will find Gobi the camel.

Use your Beak Buster to stomp on Gobi's back and water will squirt into the flower's hole. Now run back to the slope and climb back to the tree and continue to move to the right. Walk down the next path to the right and you will find the third caterpillar. Head for Mumbo's hut and you will find the fourth caterpillar waiting just outside.

Return to the large central tree and climb up to the start of the steep slope cut into the side of the tree. Turn to your right and jump onto the leaf and then jump from leaf to leaf around the tree to the right. On the platform at the top of this leaf climb you will find the first summer Jiggy.

Jigsaw Piece 4
Return down the leaves to the start of the steep slope cut into the side of the tree and climb up to the top. On your left and you will see a thin branch which splits into two, follow the left hand branch and you will find the fifth caterpillar on a leaf to your right. Head back to the tree and begin to climb up the tree to the Bee Hive. Use your Talon Trot to run onto the top of the hive and then use your Beak Buster to break a hole in the top. Drop down into the hive and then the Zubba's will attack you and try to sting you! Stand on the platform in the centre of the hive and activate your Shield move to kill all the bees as they attack you. When all the bees are dead you can collect the next golden jigsaw piece.

Jigsaw Piece 5
Exit the Bee hive and then jump around the platforms cut into the tree to the left. Climb all the way to the top of this section and then head towards the tree house to your left. Grab the sixth caterpillar from the ground in front of you and then carefully enter the tree house. On a platform in the far left hand corner you will find the next summer Jiggy. To collect this Jiggy, leap over to the corner platform with the extra life and then leap across the back of the tree house to grab this golden puzzle piece.

Now drop down to the platform below the house and follow the wooden bridge around the tree to the Squirrel's house. Keep moving around the tree until you arrive at Eyrie's nest, then feed the little chick the five caterpillars you have collected. Eyrie will begin to grow and then will fall asleep again. Make your way to the bottom of the tree and then leave this area and head for the next season.

Jigsaw Piece 6
From the door, head to the right and dive into the water and head for the Beaver's house. Providing you broke the rock in front of

the entrance in the summer season you will be able to swim into the Beaver's house and collect the first autumn Jiggy.

Jigsaw Piece 7
Now exit Gnawty's house and swim round the pool to the left. Jump out of the water near the flower and then dash past the bull and jump over the tiny fence. Gobi the camel is still here, so jump onto his back and use your Beak Buster move to stomp on his hump. As you do this Gobi will squirt more water into the flower's hole, the plant will grow to full height and the next autumn Jiggy will appear at the top. To collect this golden puzzle piece, climb up the tree to the Bee hive and then drop down over the edge and land on top of this beautiful flower.

Jigsaw Piece 8
Now climb back up the tree to the squirrel's house where you will find Nabnut outside searching for acorns. He needs six more acorns before he can settle down for the winter, so search the platforms around the house and retrieve the six acorns.

Give these acorns to Nabnut and he will reward you with the next golden puzzle piece. Now continue to climb up the central tree and you will find the winter switch near Eyrie's nest. Use your Beak Buster to activate this switch and the door to the winter season will now open. Head to Eyrie's nest and feed the eagle ten juicy caterpillars. The Eagle will grow to almost full size. Now carefully make your way back down the tree and head for the last season.

Jigsaw Piece 9
From the doorway, use your Talon Trot to dash over to the left; avoiding the snowman and heading for the flying disc in the centre. Use the disc to launch yourself into the air and then fly around the tree using your Beak Bomb attack to destroy the annoying snowmen. Now fly up to Eyrie's nest and speak to the fully grown eagle and he will show you how he has learnt to fly. Let the eagle take off and he will fly past and drop the ninth Jiggy into his empty nest to say thanks for all the help you have given him through the seasons.

Nintendo 64 A-Z of Cheats Volume 2

Jigsaw Piece 10 (Jinjos)
Now make your way back down the tree and head for the flying disc near Mumbo's hut. Launch yourself into the air and land on top of Mumbo's Hut where you will find the first Jinjo in need of rescuing.

Now exit the winter season and head back to autumn where you will find the next Jinjo waiting on the top of a pile of leaves near the blooming plant. Quickly rescue this Jinjo and then head for summer entrance. From the doorway, run around to the left and follow the line of the wall and you will find the third Jinjo right in the corner almost hidden in the long grass. Dash past the bees and offer this little guy some assistance and then leave the summer season and head back to spring to find the last two Jinjos.

Head to the right, then jump into the water and swim around to the right until you find a slope joining the centre tree. Walk up this slope and the run around the tree to the left and head for Mumbo's Hut. Have Mumbo change you back into Bee form, then fly up to the bee hive. Enter the bee hive and you will find the fourth Jinjo standing on top of the honeycombs waiting to be rescued.

Help this little fellow and then fly out of the bee hive and fly up the tree to the door at the top. In the venus flytrap opposite this door waits the fifth and final Jinjo. Fly through this plant and free the last Jinjo and you will be rewarded with the tenth and final Jiggy on this level.

Click Clock Wood Secret Switch
In the season of winter use the flying disc in front of Mumbo's hut to take off and then fly up destroying the snowball throwing snowmen. On a platform near the squirrels house you will find the secret witch switch for this level. Use your Beak Buster move to activate this switch and the last Gruntilda's Lair Jiggy will appear at the top of the tree just outside this level.

Level 10: Gruntilda's Lair

Jigsaw Piece 1
Enter Gruntilda's Lair and you will see a picture of the witch on the wall

in front of you. Turn to your left and jump up the platforms against the wall, and you will find the first Gruntilda's Lair Jiggy. Place this into the first puzzle and the door to Mumbo's Mountain will open.

Jigsaw Piece 2
Activate the secret witch switch in Mumbo's Mountain and the second Gruntilda's Lair Jiggy will appear on top of Mumbo's Mountain. To collect this golden puzzle piece, enter the level and visit the shaman so he can turn you back into a termite. Now exit the level and use the tiny termite to climb the hill and grab the second Jiggy.

Jigsaw Piece 3
Activate the secret witch switch in Treasure Trove Cove and the third Gruntilda's Lair Jiggy will get fired out of the cannon at the entrance to this level. Exit this level and then jump onto the cannon to climb up onto the ship to the left. Now continue across the rear wall and you will find the third Gruntilda's Lair Jiggy on the highest platform.

Jigsaw Piece 4
Activate the secret witch switch in Clanker's Cavern and the eyes of the witch portrait will pop up. Use your Beak Buster to stomp on both the raised eyes and the fourth Gruntilda's Lair Jiggy will be yours.

Jigsaw Piece 5
Activate the secret witch switch inside one of the tall hut platforms and the top of the huge witch statue will blow up! To collect this Jiggy head to the golden pot and then use your Beak Barge to knock down the wall to the left. At the end of the passage you will find a special switch, so use your Beak Buster to activate this switch and a shock jump disc will appear near the golden pot. Now use this shock jump disc to jump into the pot and you will fall through a hole in the floor and down through the blown up witches hat. You will find the fifth Gruntilda's Lair Jiggy at the bottom.

Nintendo 64 A-Z of Cheats Volume 2

Jigsaw Piece 6
Use your Beak Bomb attack to destroy all the small snowmen around Freezeezy Peak and you will find the next secret witch switch. Activate this switch and the next Gruntilda's Lair Jiggy will appear on top of the advent calendar.

Exit the level and run back to the room with all the cobwebs, then shoot the cobwebs with your eggs until they break and disappear. Now return to the bottom of the advent calendar and use the shock jump disc to jump up to the next level.

Run across to the left and you will find a blue switch and a pair of running shoes. Activate the switch, grab the running shoes and dash for the flying pad in the room with the cobwebs. As soon as your feet touch the flying disc, press A to launch yourself into the air and then fly back to the advent calendar to grab the sixth Jiggy.

Jigsaw Piece 7
Activate the witch switch in Gobi's Valley and the next Gruntilda's Lair Jiggy will appear near the golden pot. Exit the level and then run back to the pot and use the shock jump disc revolving around the pot, to jump up and grab this high up golden Jiggy.

Jigsaw Piece 8
Activate the witch switch high in Mad Monster Mansion and the next Gruntilda's Lair Jiggy will appear in the eye socket of the large witch head statue. Now exit the level and return to the advent calendar and climb back up to the blue switch. Activate the switch, grab the running shoes and dash for the flying disc in the next room. As soon as your feet touch the disc, launch yourself into the air and then use your Beak Bomb attack to bust open the eye socket on the statue. Now just fly into the socket and grab the eighth Jigsaw piece.

Jigsaw Piece 9
Activate the switch on the tall platform at the back of the ship in Rusty Bucket Bay and the next Gruntilda's Lair jiggy will appear on a platform above the first pool. Now leave the level and stomp on the switch inside the rare box to raise the water level to the

right height. Swim back to the first pool, swim up to the surface, and leap out the water onto the ledge. Here you can collect the ninth Gruntilda's Lair Jiggy.

Jigsaw Piece 10
In the winter season of Click Clock Wood, activate the witch switch and the last Gruntilda's Lair Jiggy will appear on top of the tree outside the level. To collect this golden puzzle piece, enter the season of spring and have Mumbo change you back into a bee.   Now exit the level and fly up to the top of the tree to grab the tenth and final Gruntilda's Lair Jiggy.

Grunty's Furnace Fun
Climb the tree near the entrance to Click Clock Wood and open the next Note Door. You will need to have collected at least 765 musical notes up to this point before you can pass through this special door. Follow the passage to the end and then jump onto the central platform to be whisked into Grunty's Furnace Fun.

Banjo-Kazooie
Step onto this square and you will be asked a question relating to the game. This question could be about any of the characters or levels that you have passed through whilst playing the game. You are offered a choice of three different answers and you must choose the correct answer within the ten second time limit.

Visual Question
Step onto the Visual question square and you must answer a question regarding to the whereabouts of certain items or characters. The pictures you will be shown are normally close-ups and so it can be tricky to pinpoint the level it relates to.

Audio Question
The Audio question squares will test your knowledge of the level music and voices of the characters you have met. Listen carefully to the tune or the voice and then highlight the correct answer from your choice of three. If you answer the question correctly you can

proceed across the game board, but if you fail you will lose an energy piece.

Gruntilda Question
Step onto the Gruntilda question square and you will have to answer a question about your evil hostess. If you have spoken to Brentilda throughout the game you should have no trouble with these questions. However if you have not spoken to Gruntilda's sister you will just have to guess.

Joker Question
These special squares will reward you with two joker cards if you can answer the question correctly. The jokers will enable you to skip certain game squares by pressing the B button, which can help when approaching the final stretch. The question could be on almost any game related subject, and as before you will have a choice of three different answers.

Deadly Question
The deadly question square is the most difficult square on the entire game board. This could be from any of the categories of questions, so it is a bit like a lucky dip. The major problem with these squares is that you will be flipped off the game board and into the lava if you answer the question incorrectly. Tread carefully on these squares or use a joker to pass them safely.

Timed Challenge
When you step onto a timed challenge square you must complete the task set in the time limit allowed. These challenges could be any of the timed challenges you have competed in previously. Complete the set task within the time limit and you will be able to proceed to the next game square. If you fail in the challenge you will lose an energy piece and will have to attempt the challenge again.

Banjo-Kazooie - The Final Battle

Climb the stairs to the right and then open the next note door on the right. You will need to have collected at least 810 musical notes to break the spell on this door. Enter the room on the other side and you will see another incomplete picture on the wall ahead. Fill in the missing pieces and the large door to your left will open; revealing a cauldron called Dingpot and four more note doors. Jump into the cauldron in the centre and Dingpot will fire you up to the roof where the final battle will take place.

At the start of the final battle Gruntilda will be flying around on her broomstick. As she zooms towards you, quickly side-step her attack and then turn to face the next attack run. After a couple of attempts to knock you over, Gruntilda's broomstick will splutter and stop momentarily. Quickly dash over to the witch and use your Rat-A-Tat attack to whack the witch.

Now run away to dodge the incoming fireball attack, and repeat until Gruntilda moves to the side of the castle. Quickly dash to the side of the castle and duck down behind the wall to evade her fireball attacks. Now after the fourth fireball, leap onto the side ledge and shoot the witch with your eggs. Each time you manage to hit the witch with your attack she will move around the castle and start throwing fireballs again.

Splat the witch on all four sides of the building and she will then take to the skies for a second time. Wait until the flying disc appears on the roof, and then use it to launch yourself into the air. Now fly around the skies and use your Beak Bomb attack to wallop the witch whenever she is still. When you have hit the witch four times she will initiate her shield which you will not be able to penetrate.

Drop down to the castle roof and four small Jinjo statues will appear in the corners. Feed the statues with eggs and one by one they will fly up and attack the evil witch. Keep on the move all the time as the witch will up her fireball attacks. Once all four corner Jinjos have inflicted their damage on Gruntilda, the final Jinjo will appear in the centre of the roof. Dash around the central statue and fire eggs into the four holes on each side. It will take a few eggs in each hole to activate this final Jinjo, so keep firing eggs until the hole is sealed. Once you have filled all four holes the final

Jinjo will join the other four Jinjos and knock the witch over the side of the castle. Congratulations you have rescued Tooty and destroyed the evil Witch.

BIO FREAKS

One Hit Fatalities
Minatek
Move in close and press Towards, Away, C Left + C Down.

Zipperhead
Towards, Away, Away + C Right. The first time you'll take one arm off, the second time the other arm. Finally move in close to take off the head.

Ssapo
Move in close and press Towards, Away, Away + C Up + C Right.

PsyClown
Move in close and press Towards, Away, Away + C Left + C Down.

Sabotage
Towards, Away, Away + C Up. The first time you'll take one arm off, then the other arm. Finally move to about three steps away and take off the head.

BullzEye
Move in close and press Towards, Away, Away + C Up.

Delta
Move in close and press Towards, Away, Away + C Down

Purge
Away, Towards, Towards + C Up + C Right.

Taunt
To taunt your opponent hold C Left and C Right.

First-Person Perspective
During a fight hold Away on the pad and press Start. To switch back hold Down on the control pad and press Start.

BLAST CORPS (US)

Deadly Doors!
Can't be bothered to mess about with all that tedious precision destruction? This cheat will help you out no end. Just drive your vehicle right alongside a building and use the Z button. Normally this would make your driver get out, but if the door is blocked he'll just shout at you. Keep holding the Z button, and a few moments later the obstruction will magically explode!

BUST-A-MOVE 2

Extra Levels
On the title screen tap L, Up, R, Down. If you've entered the code correctly a Bubble Bobble baddie will appear on the bottom right of the screen. To access the new levels select puzzle mode, which will have the words 'Another World' underneath.

Hidden Characters (Puzzle Mode)
On the Puzzle Mode screen before you select your first destination press Left, Left, Up, Down, L, R, L, R, L + R. This accesses a character selection screen allowing you to switch from Bub to Bob or one of the bosses.

Bonus Characters In Vs Mode
First enable the "Another World" code on the title screen

(press L, Up, R, Down). Then choose Player vs Player mode on the game select screen and you'll be asked to pick your character. The further you've gone in Player vs Computer mode, the more characters you will be able to access.

CHAMELEON TWIST

Take on bosses early
Pick up twenty crowns on each level and a box marked with a question mark will pop up on the level selection screen. This option will let you take on any of the level bosses without needing to play through the level each time. The markings on the door let you know which boss you are about to fight.

Infinite Health
If you're running low on health then follow these simple steps to gain infinite health!
1. Save the game to one of the data slots.
2. Exit the game.
3. Load the game and have full energy.

CHOPPER ATTACK

Alien Disruptor
To kit your chopper out with an alien disruptor weapon you'll need to beat level seven on Expert.

CLAYFIGHTER 63 1/3

Cheat Mode
On the character selection screen, hold L and press Up, Right, Left, Down, B, A. The options screen should now display a cheat selection option.

Fight As Dr Kiln
On the character selection screen hold L and press B, Left, Up, Right, Down, A.

Fight As Sumo Santa
On the character selection screen, hold L and press A, Down, Right, Up, Left, B.

Fight As Boogerman
On the character selection screen hold L and press C Up, C Right, C Left, C Down, B, A.

Fight As A Random Character
On the character selection screen, hold L and R.

CRUISN' USA (US)

Secret Vehicles
If you're fed up with this game (and who could blame you?), holding down the Top, Left and Bottom C (yellow) buttons on the controller while you are on the vehicle select screen will allow you to access the police car, Jeep and school bus. It's not much, but it might let you eke a little more value from this hideous game.

Nintendo 64 A-Z of Cheats Volume 2

DisembodiedHead
Get a Hot Time to bring up the Hot Times screen. After inputting your initials, go to the bottom of the list and hold left for over 30 seconds. A head will then appear on the conveyor belt, a bizarre trick which allows you to access the cheat mode.

Lights & Siren
If you like the police car or school bus cheat you'll no doubt be eager be to activate the flashing lights on the school bus and the siren/flashing lights of the police car. Perform the Disembodied Head trick above, then during a race press Brake, Brake, Accelerate in quick succession. Timed correctly, it will activate your vehicle's special feature. To deactivate, release accelerate.

Nitrous Boost
Perform the Disembodied Head trick above, then during a race press Brake, Brake, Brake, Accelerate, Brake, Accelerate. Whenever you pass a checkpoint, you can use this cheat to get a nitrous boost. (This cheat only works on the fourth level.)

Level Access
This cheat lets you access levels not normally accessible from the level select screen (except for Washington DC which you still have play through the game for). Go to the course select screen, then hold down the following button combinations:

Golden Gate Park – Left C, Bottom C and L

Indiana – Top C, Right C and L

San Francisco – Right C, Bottom C and L

DARK RIFT (US)

Play As Bosses
Completed the game with the eight standard characters already? No problem. Just enter these codes on the title screen to access the two hidden boss characters!

Sonork
L, R, C Up, C Down, C Left, C Right

Demitron
A, B, R, L, C Down, C Up

View All Endings
Want to view each character's ending without the hassle of having to play through the entire game? Then enter these codes on the title screen.

Aaron
Up, C Left, R, Right, Down, R, R, C Left

Demonica
Up, C Left, R, Right, Down, R, R, C Up

Demitron
Up, C Left, R, Right, Down, L, L, C Down

Eve
Up, C Left, R, Right, Down, R, R, C Right

Gore
Up, C Left, R, Right, Down, R, R, C Down

Morphix
Up, C Left, R, Right, Down, R, R, B

Nintendo 64 A-Z of Cheats Volume 2

Niiki
Up, C Left, R, Right, Down, R, R, A

Scarlet
Up, C Left, R, Right, Down, L, L, C Left

Sonork
Up, C Left, R, Right, Down, L, L, C Up

Zenmuron
Up, C Left, R, Right, Down, L, L, C Right

DIDDY KONG RACING

Turbo start
Just a taster of a cheat for this excellent new racer – to get a turbo start, press and hold the accelerator as the words 'Get Ready' fade out. If you want a super turbo, which jets you away in a blast of blue flame, press the button a fraction of a second before the words fade entirely. Who needs Thrust SSC?

Magic Codes
Enter the codes below on the Magic Codes screen for various helpful (and not so helpful) effects. Once the codes have been entered, they can be turned on or off by accessing the 'code list' screen. Some of them will work in adventure mode, others will only have an effect in tracks mode.

JOINTVENTURE – Co-operative two player adventure.
DOUBLEVISION – Everyone can select the same player.
FREEFORALL – Maximum power-up on pickups.
FREEFRUIT – Start race with ten bananas.

VITAMINB – No limit to number of banana power-ups.
ZAPTHEZIPPERS – Remove zippers from the track.
NOYELLOWSTUFF – No bananas on track.
BYEBYEBALLOONS – No balloons on track.
TIMETOLOSE – Ultimate AI characters.
BOGUSBANANAS – Bananas reduce speed.
BODYARMOR – All balloons are yellow shield balloons.
ROCKETFUEL – All balloons are blue boost balloons.
BOMBSAWAY – All balloons are red rocket balloons.
OPPOSITESATTRACT – All balloons are magnetic.
TOXICOFFENDER – All balloons are green drop behind.
ARNOLD – Larger characters.
TEENYWEENIES – Smaller characters.
OFFROAD – Four-wheel drive for more speed.
BLABBERMOUTH – Characters burble incoherently.
JUKEBOX – Music menu.
WHODIDTHIS – View the credits without winning.

Play As Drumstick

To access the cartoon characters' fastest racer, you'll first need to get all the amulet pieces from both amulets and the four gold trophies. Then return to the central area where all the frogs are and look for the little green fellow sporting some red feathers. Run him over to enable Drumstick.

Play As TT

You'll need to beat the small clock-like fellow in every race on time-trial mode. You'll know whether you've done it because you'll see his ghost as you race, and if you do it he'll tell you to 'try the next race'. Beat all TT's times, and you'll be able to play as him! Oh, and it's not at all easy...

General Hints

The different characters in Diddy Kong Racing vary in weight, speed, acceleration and handling. Here they are in ascending order of heaviness, with their characteristics:
   Different characters are useful in different situations. The

Nintendo 64 A-Z of Cheats Volume 2

heavy characters, for example, are slower on rough terrain, like grass and sand, but they are not so easily knocked out of the way by opponent vehicles. The lighter characters on the other hand move faster on rough terrain, but have a nasty habit of getting knocked away from zippers and balloons just as they are about to get them due to an opponent colliding with them.

Characters

Character	Top speed	Reached in	Handling
Pipsy the Mouse	55	2.5 secs	Superb
Tiptup the Turtle	55	3 secs	Superb
Conker the Squirrel	55	3 secs	Very Good
Diddy Kong	55	3 secs	Very Good
Timber the Tiger	57.5	3 secs	Very Good
Bumper the Badger	57.5	3 secs	Good
Banjo the Bear	57.5	3 secs	Good
Krunch the Crocodile	60	6 secs	Poor

DOOM 64

Level Codes
Be Gentle!
Level 02: CDP8 9BJ2 68ZT SVK?
Level 03: CXM8 9BJY 681T JVK?
Level 04: DDK8 9BJT 683S 9VK?
Level 05: DXH8 9BJP 685S 1VK?
Level 06: FDF8 9BJK 687S SVK?
Level 07: FXC8 9BJF 689S JVK?
Level 08: GD?8 9BC? 69BR ?BK?
Level 09: GX88 9BC6 69DR 2BK?
Level 10: HD68 9BC2 69GR TBK?
Level 11: HX48 9BCY 69JR KBK?
Level 12: JD28 9BCT 69LQ ?BK?
Level 13: JX08 9BCP 69NQ 2BK?
Level 14: KDY8 9BCK 69QQ TBK?

Level 15: KXW8 9BCF 69SQ KBK?
Level 16: LFT8 9BB? 69VP ?VK?
Level 17: LYR8 9BB6 69XP 2VK?
Level 18: MFP8 9BB2 69ZP TVK?
Level 19: MYM8 9BBY 691P KVK?
Level 20: NFK8 9BBT 693N ?VK?
Level 21: NYH8 9BBP 695N 2VK?
Level 22: PFF8 9BBK 697N TVK?
Level 23: PYC8 9BBF 699N KVK?
Level 24: QF?8 9BF? 6?BM ?BK?
Level 25: QY88 9BF6 6?DM 2BK?
Level 26: RF68 9BF2 6?GM TBK?
Level 27: RY48 9BFY 6?JM KBK?
Level 28: SF28 9BFT 6?LL ?BK?
Level 29: SY08 9BFP 6?NL 2BK?
Level 30: TFY8 9BFK 6?QL TBK?
Level 31: TYW8 9BFF 6?SL KBK?
Level 32: VBT8 9BD? 6?VK 9VK?

Bring It On!
Level 02: CJPR 9BJ1 68Z? QVK?
Level 03: C1MR 9BJX 681? GVK?
Level 04: DJKR 9BJS 6839 7VK?
Level 05: D1HR 9BJN 6859 ZVK?
Level 06: FJFR 9BJJ 6879 QVK?
Level 07: F1CR 9BJD 6899 GVK?
Level 08: GJ?R 9BC9 69B8 8BK?
Level 09: G18R 9BC5 69D8 0BK?
Level 10: HJ6R 9BC1 69G8 RBK?
Level 11: H14R 9BCX 69J8 HBK?
Level 12: JJ2R 9BCS 69L7 8BK?
Level 13: J10R 9BCN 69N7 0BK?
Level 14: KJYR 9BCJ 69Q7 RBK?
Level 15: K1WR 9BCD 69S7 HBK?
Level 16: LKTR 9BB9 69V6 8VK?
Level 17: L2RR 9BB5 69X6 0VK?
Level 18: MKPR 9BB1 69Z6 RVK?

Nintendo 64 A-Z of Cheats Volume 2

Level 19: M2MR 9BBX 6916 HVK?
Level 20: NKKR 9BBS 6935 8VK?
Level 21: N2HR 9BBN 6955 0VK?
Level 22: PKFR 9BBJ 6975 RVK?
Level 23: P2CR 9BBD 6995 HVK?
Level 24: QK?R 9BF9 6?B4 8BK?
Level 25: Q28R 9BF5 6?D4 0BK?
Level 26: RK6R 9BF1 6?G4 RBK?
Level 27: R24R 9BFX 6?J4 HBK?
Level 28: SK2R 9BFS 6?L3 8BK?
Level 29: S20R 9BFN 6?N3 0BK?
Level 30: TKYR 9BFJ 6?Q3 RBK?
Level 31: T2WR 9BFD 6?S3 HBK?
Level 32: VGTR 9BD9 6?V2 7VK?

I Own Doom!
Level 02: CNN8 9BJ0 680T NVK?
Level 03: C5L8 9BJW 682T DVK?
Level 04: DNJ8 9BJR 684S 5VK?
Level 05: D5G8 9BJM 686S XVK?
Level 06: FND8 9BJH 688S NVK?
Level 07: F5B8 9BJC 68?S DVK?
Level 08: GN98 9BC8 69CR 6BK?
Level 09: G578 9BC4 69FR YBK?
Level 10: HN58 9BC0 69HR PBK?
Level 11: H538 9BCW 69KR FBK?
Level 12: JN18 9BCR 69MQ 6BK?
Level 13: J5Z8 9BCM 69PQ YBK?
Level 14: KNX8 9BCH 69RQ PBK?
Level 15: K5V8 9BCC 69TQ FBK?
Level 16: LPS8 9BB8 69WP 6VK?
Level 17: L6Q8 9BB4 69YP YVK?
Level 18: MPN8 9BB0 690P PVK?
Level 19: M6L8 9BBW 692P FVK?
Level 20: NPJ8 9BBR 694N 6VK?
Level 21: N6G8 9BBM 696N YVK?
Level 22: PPD8 9BBH 698N PVK?

Level 23: P6B8 9BBC 69?N FVK?
Level 24: QP98 9BF8 6?CM 6BK?
Level 25: Q678 9BF4 6?FM YBK?
Level 26: RP58 9BF0 6?HM PBK?
Level 27: R638 9BFW 6?KM FBK?
Level 28: SP18 9BFR 6?ML 6BK?
Level 29: S6Z8 9BFM 6?PL YBK?
Level 30: TPX8 9BFH 6?RL PBK?
Level 31: T6V8 9BFC 6?TL FBK?
Level 32: VLS8 9BD8 6?WK 5VK?

Watch Me Die!
Level 02: CSNR 9BJZ 680? LVK?
Level 03: C9LR 9BJV 682? BVK?
Level 04: DSJR 9BJQ 6849 3VK?
Level 05: D9GR 9BJL 6869 VVK?
Level 06: FSDR 9BJG 6889 LVK?
Level 07: F9BR 9BJB 68?9 BVK?
Level 08: GS9R 9BC7 69C8 4BK?
Level 09: G97R 9BC3 69F8 WBK?
Level 10: HS5R 9BCZ 69H8 MBK?
Level 11: H93R 9BCV 69K8 CBK?
Level 12: JS1R 9BCQ 69M7 4BK?
Level 13: J9ZR 9BCL 69P7 WBK?
Level 14: KSXR 9BCG 69R7 MBK?
Level 15: K9VR 9BCB 69T7 CBK?
Level 16: LTSR 9BB7 69W6 4VK?
Level 17: L?QR 9BB3 69Y6 WVK?
Level 18: MTNR 9BBZ 6906 MVK?
Level 19: M?LR 9BBV 6926 CVK?
Level 20: NTJR 9BBQ 6945 4VK?
Level 21: N?GR 9BBL 6965 WVK?
Level 22: PTDR 9BBG 6985 MVK?
Level 23: P?BR 9BBB 69?5 CVK?
Level 24: QT9R 9BF7 6?C4 4BK?
Level 25: Q?7R 9BF3 6?F4 WBK?
Level 26: RT5R 9BFZ 6?H4 MBK?
Level 27: R?3R 9BFV 6?K4 CBK?

Level 28: ST1R 9BFQ 6?M3 4BK?
Level 29: S?ZR 9BFL 6?P3 WBK?
Level 30: TTXR 9BFG 6?R3 MBK?
Level 31: T?VR 9BFB 6?T3 CBK?
Level 32: VQSR 9BD7 6?W2 3VK?

Ultimate Cheat Code
?TJL BDFW BFGV JVVB
Enter this code and start the game, then pause to see a 'Features' option. From here you can access all levels, view all maps, obtain all weapons and ammo, give yourself maximum health and even make yourself invincible!

DUKE NUKEM

The bad news is that we couldn't get these cheats to work on the UK version of the game – those programming types up at Eurocom must have changed things! Still, if you've got the American version of this great blaster, you can still try them out for size!

Enable Cheat Menu
This is the first thing you have to do – none of the other cheats here will work until the cheat mode is active. On the main menu screen, enter Left, Left, L, L, Right, Right, Left, Left.

Level Select
First enable the Cheat menu, then on the main menu press R, L, R, C Down, Right, Up, Left, C Up. You'll hear a monster howl if you entered the code correctly, and it will then be possible to select any level you want from the cheat menu during play.

Invincibility
When the cheat menu is active, press R seven times to make Duke even more nails than usual!

No Enemies
When the cheat menu is active, enter L, C Left, Left, R, C Right, Right, Left, Left, Right to play the game with no monsters! Where's the fun in that?

All Items
When the cheat menu is active, enter R, C Right, Right, L, C Left, Left, C Right, Right in order to be able to obtain all special items at will.

EXTREME G BIGG5 D

Fergus Mode Antigrav Fisheye
Enter FERGUS in the shoot-'em-up mode to replace all the drones with the bouncing, grinning head of former Probe Software boss Fergus McGovern!

Quit While You're Ahead Roller
If you can't be bothered to run a whole race, enter RA50 as your name. During a race, if you quit you'll be awarded points based on your position at the time.

F1 POLE POSITION

Secret Car
Complete the entire game, succeed in becoming the world champion and save the game to a control pak. Restart the game, and when the "please wait while loading" message is displayed, press the A and B buttons together. Once the game has loaded, go to the car selection screen and you will have access to a secret car!

Arsnal nitroid

Infinite Fuel
Keep running out of fuel in Grand Prix mode? For unlimited gas, go to the settings menu and set the initial amount of fuel to just 10%. You'll find that although the gauge will flash on the red, you'll never run out, and the added bonus is that your car will be much lighter and so have far better acceleration!

FIFA: ROAD TO WORLD CUP

Edit Players And Colours
While on the EA Sports screen, enter A, B, A, B, B, B, A, Z.

Noisy Crowd
During the game, push various directions on the d-pad and the crowd will hurl abuse at the other team!

Ghost Players
Choose Slovakia as your team and enter LASKO on the player edit screen.

Different Scoring Animation
Enter C Left, C Right, C Up, or C Down directly after a goal for a variety of scoring animations.

Invisible Players
Choose Sheffield Wednesday as your team and enter WAYNE on the player edit screen.

Small Players
Choose Vancouver as your team and enter KERRY on the player edit screen.

Big Heads
Choose Vancouver as your team and enter ANATOLI on the player edit screen.

Black & White Mode
Choose Canada as your team and enter MARC on the player edit screen.

No Stadium
Increase the speed of the game by choosing any team and entering CATCH22 on the player edit screen.

FIGHTER'S DESTINY

Fight As Boro
Complete the game in Vs Mode on the Easy setting.

Fight As The Joker
Complete the game in Vs Mode with Pierre. Select Survival Mode. Defeat all 100 opponents. The Joker will be available on the character selection screen.

Fight As The Master
Complete the game in Vs Mode with Ryuji. Select Master Challenge Mode and defeat all 12 opponents (four Jokers and eight Masters). The Master will be available on the character selection screen.

Fight As Robert
Complete the game in Vs Mode with Valerie. Select Fastest Mode. Defeat all four opponents in a combined time of under one minute. Robert the Robot will be available on the character selection screen.

Fight As Ushi
Complete the game in Vs Mode with Abdul. Select Rodeo

Mode. Remain undefeated for at least one minute. Ushi the cow will be available on the character selection screen in two choices of colours.

FORSAKEN

Unlimited Nitro
On the opening screen press B, B, R, Up, Left, Down, C Up, C Left.

Psychedelic Mode
On the opening screen press A, R, Left, Right, Down, C Up, C Left, C Down.

Wireframe Mode
On the opening screen press L, L, R, Z, Left, Right, C Up, C Right.

Gore Mode
On the opening screen press Z, Down, C Up, C Left, C Left, C Left , C Left, C Down.

Turbo Crazy Mode
On the opening screen press B, B, R, Up, Left, Down, C Up, C Left.

Secret Characters
Hidden within the game are eight secret characters. If you manage to find them and kill them they will then be accessible from the Biker select screen. There are eight secret characters in total: Septre, Ex-Cop, Jo, Nubia, Cerbero, Mephistofun, HK-5, and Dr Nepenthe (Nutta). If you've unlocked Battle Mode you can also access the characters by killing them on one of the eight battle mode levels.They also sometimes appear in multiplayer mode as one of the CPU opponents (if you have them activated).

GOLDENEYE

Lovers of doing things the easy way are going to be disappointed – there are no push-button cheats for Goldeneye, as you have to completing certain levels within tight time limits. Also, you can only use the cheats on levels you have already completed (pick them from the 'cheat' menu). Difficulty is the setting you must be playing on: Agent (A), Secret Agent (SA) or 00 Agent (00).

Secret Levels And Characters

Complete the game on Agent level to access the secret characters in deathmatch mode (including Jaws, Mayday, Oddjob and Baron Samedi). Complete the game on Secret Agent level to open up the hidden Aztec level.
Complete the game on 00 Agent level to open up the Egyptian Crypt level. Beat this on 00 level to access the 007 mode, which includes a level editor!
Also, once the Bunker 2, Archive and Caverns levels have been beaten in Agent mode, they will become accessible in multiplayer games.

Extra Weapons

Beat the final mission (including the secret levels) on each of the difficulty levels to receive a permanent new weapon.
Agent: Cougar Magnum
Secret Agent: Moonraker laser
00 Agent: Golden Gun

Level	Cheat	Diff	Time
Dam	Paintball	SA	2:40
Facility	Invincibility	00	2:05
Runway	Donkey Kong	A	5:00
Surface	Grenade launcher	SA	3:30
Bunker	Rocket launcher	00	4:00

Nintendo 64 A-Z of Cheats Volume 2

Silo	Turbo Bond	A	3:00
Frigate	No radar	SA	4:30
Surface 2	Mini Bond	00	4:15
Bunker 2	Throwing knives	A	1:30
Statue Park	Turbo animation	SA	3:15
Archives	Invisibility	00	1:20
Streets	Rockets	A	1:45
Depot	Slow animation	SA	1:30
Train	Silver PP7	00	5:25
Jungle	Hunting knives	A	3:45
Control	Infinite ammo	SA	10:00
Caverns	Twin RCP90s	00	9:30
Cradle	Golden PP7	A	2:15
Aztec	Moonraker lasers	SA	9:00
Crypt	All weapons	00	6:00

Extra Players In Deathmatch

Go to the character selection screen. Move your cursor along all the way right to the last character available (it'll either be Mishkin or the Moonraker Elite). Once you're there, enter the following code.

Hold L & R & C Left and release.
Hold L & C Up and release.
Hold L & R & Left on D-pad and release.
Hold L & Right on D-pad and release.
Hold R & Down on D-pad and release.
Hold L & R & C Left and release.
Hold L & C Up and release.
Hold L & R & Right on D-pad and release.
Hold L & R & C Down and release.
Hold L & Down on D-pad and release.

You will now be able to access a whole host of new characters, including the programmers, a terrorist and a biker dude!

Destroy The Flag

When taking part in a flag-tag multiplayer game, if you're

using some form of explosive weapons, there is a neat way to win the game easily. Get the flag, then after you've had possession of it for a short time, blow yourself up. The flag will be destroyed and thus no-one else will be able to pick it up – so you will win!

Hover Mode
Activate the Tiny Bond cheat (by completing the Surface 2 level in under 4:15 on 00 level), then stand somewhere high up, such as at the top of some stairs or a ladder. Crouch down to make yourself even lower, and very slowly walk off the high area. You'll find that you don't move down the stairs, but instead walk into space! By moving very slowly, it's actually possible to walk for quite a distance. A good place to try this is the Dam level. Unfortunately you can't float over obstacles, so there's still no way to reach the mystery complex on the far side of the reservoir...

Hidden Weapons
On the Train level, blow up the last box at the far end of the start room for a hidden RCP-90.
On the Water Caverns level, blow up the boxes in the radio room. One of the boxes will spew out more boxes. Keep blowing them up and eventually you'll get two assault rifles.

Kill People During Cut Sequences
Not so much a cheat, more a fun little aside this. Play Goldeneye using the two control pad 'Domino' setting, and at the end of each level during the animation sequences you'll be able to shoot people using the second pad! This is particularly satisfying on levels where you are captured at the end, as you can mow down your captors.

Paintbrush mode - Single Player
Start the game and make your way to the top of the first guard tower without collecting any other weapons. You can kill the guards if you want, just don't pick up their weapons.

Nintendo 64 A-Z of Cheats Volume 2

At the top of the tower, press A to put away your gun so that you're unarmed and pick up the sniper rifle. Now press A three times fast to obtain the mysterious weapon. The only catches are that if you press A again you'll lose the weapon, and that it's not much good anyway!

Paintbrush mode - Multi Player
Start a game on any level with sniper rifles selected as your special weapon. Now (any player can do this) go pick up a sniper rifle without collecting any other weapon. When you've got one, press A twice fast.

WALKTHROUGH

Mission 1: Arkangelsk
Level Guide Mission 1.1
Right Bond, get that vodka martini out of your face and start behaving like a member of Her Majesty's elite. Whichever difficulty level you're playing on you will need to first deal with the guard standing before the bridge (head shots remember – it will save ammo later on) and then creep over to the base of the first watchtower. Take out the guards here and then pick up the sniper rifle from the top of the tower. Use this (and the extra zoom on the top yellow button) to take out both sentries in the tunnel.

Follow the road round to the next tower, but make sure you don't take hits from the two guards on the ground and the two inside the bunker. Instead of getting into a firefight, it is better to leg it straight to the tower where you can use the sniper rifle to get a higher vantage point. The two in the bunker can now be blasted.

With the area cleared, head on over to the lorry and press the panel on the wall to send it through to the security gate. You will now need to press the second gate panel to releases the second gate and let the truck through. Use the large vehicle to hide you from the two guards – one on the left (who goes for the alarm as soon as you show your head) – and one standing near the watch tower. Kill the left one first, then take care of the other (still using the lorry as cover – duck if necessary). Now shoot the alarm on the wall of the building and enter it through the large shutter not through the gate. Inside are two guards – the Brown Shirt has a DD44.

Now, if playing as OO Agent, you must walk around the side of the building and activate your covert modem whilst facing the computer readout on the wall. Now shoot the padlock from the gate and head out onto the dam itself. The dam is a long structure which bears slightly to the left and features three watch towers on the right perimeter. Each tower has a sentry walking around the top in an anti-clockwise direction. Run along the damn until you are fairly close and shoot each guard through the eyes with the sniper rifle (very satisfying this!). Inside the room below each tower is an alarm panel, so if you are playing on Secret Agent or above, make sure you blast all three, and provided you got the one earlier, Objective 1 will be complete.

If you an Agent or Secret Agent, you can now head for the middle left side of the dam and simply walk over the edge of the right platform to complete the mission and bungee jump down to the chemical weapons facility.

However, you OO Agents have some more work to do. Once all alarms have been taken care of, make your way down to staircase C and head down to the lower dark green corridor. You will be at the end of the passage and there are no guards here. In order to make it through this section alive, you must use your side-step and strafe move to duck in and out of alcoves and shoot guards. Basically the tunnel is a series of small rooms and the 20-odd guards stay pressed up against of the walls. To get the guards, use the sniper rifle and stick your head out from the edge of a wall by holding down the Right shoulder button and press the Left yellow button. Now shoot each guard in the head, and

Nintendo 64 A-Z of Cheats Volume 2

has you progress up the passage, watch out for sneeky guards waiting in corners who only attack when you pass. Also make sure you don't stand next to any crates or barrels, as a stray enemy show will hurt you badly.

By now you will have made it right up to the control room and left a trail of bodies and devestation behind you. All well and good.

You will come to a steel door with an arrow pointing upwards. Open this and then run down the corridor; switching to your KF7 for any close-up encounters. The room at the end which houses the computer gear has five guards in it, and you must be careful not to blow everything up in the head of a battle. Better to lead them out to you. In particular, watch out for the crafty bugger who is hiding right behind one of the mainframes. With all life extinguished, approach the mainframe computer, press B and wait for the data to be backed-up. Once Objective 3 is completed, head up to the top and bungee off.

Level Guide - Mission 1.2

Not very suave circumstances for Bond to be in, but you begin this level in the air ducts above the toilets. Head left at the junction and then look through the gap in the floor panels. You can actually shoot the guard in the cubicle if you wish, then drop down and take out the one having a Jimmy in the nearby urinals. If you wait around on long enough, a scientist may appear, and if you get him, you will obtain Keycard A, which will open most of the security guards in the complex. This happens rarely though.

Proceed through the door out onto the balcony and head around the top and through a set of double doors to the stairs. Shoot the guard and once through the doors on the bottom level you will find a guard with his back to you (on OO Agent level you will find this place is alive with guards, so stay sharp). Point your gun right at the back of the stationary guard's head and put a cap in it (so to speak)! He will relinquish Keycard B which opens the door with the security console in it across the hall.

There are two guards on patrol in the hall, and three in the console room, all must be dispatched with minimum fuss if you want to enter the laboratory complex. Once you press the button and it turns from red to green in the room, you will only have a short time to reach the door on the other side of the glass or you will be locked out. Make sure you have nothing left to do in this area and move through to the secure area. Remember the Body Armour if you are playing on a lower difficulty level.

There are two guards in the locker section immediately after the security door, but you can just see their guns, so shoot them carefully before walking through the next bulkhead door. The next section has three guards standing in the middle of the corridor and they will all shoot on sight. Use the door as cover and strafe them all to death; moving forward as you do so. Luckily there are slabs of concrete on either side which you can use for cover, but still shoot their feet whilst you are safe. Cool.

On Secret Agent or above you are required to contact the double agent, Dr Doak, and the two rooms with massive gas tanks to the left and right here are possible places where he might be hiding. His position is random.

At the end of the corridor are two security doors leading to a U-shaped corridor section with two locked doors at either end. The room directly in front of you as you enter this area has four guards in it and two consoles. Each one of these panels will open the closest security door. The way to get past this is to lure the guards out of the room, rather than rushing in and getting caught in lethal crossfire.

The lower room (on the right) if you are facing the console room is a large experimentation area which might house Dr Doak if he is nowhere else, but is otherwise useless. To complete Objective one, you must enter the door on the left. Beware, there is a guard waiting by the stairs, and two more behind the boxes in the corner. Head up the stairs and take out the handful of guards here as quietly as possible to avoid rousing the ones later on.

Nintendo 64 A-Z of Cheats Volume 2

You will now find yourself in a corridor with small glass-fronted laboratories all around. Dr Doak might be one of these, and there are some guards hiding in the corner on the right behind the pillar. If you don't find Doak here, you must go back to one of the laboratories. Round the corridor are two guards with their backs to you (if you haven't already roused them with your gunplay). Take them both out like an assassin and then face the last security door. Now there are two ways through here. If you have seen Dr Doak, then you will have a Decoder which will open it for you. If not, then you can shoot loudly and no doubt a guard will open it from the other side. If this happens though, you have probably already failed the mission.

The next large room is the bottling plant where you'll meet OO6 dossing about at the bottom of the stairs. Exchange a few words and then start chucking those five remote mines at the large canisters. If you place one at a junction of four, they will take them out more efficiently.

Do this quickly because General Ourumov will soon send in a battalion of crack troops who surround OO6 and execute him. With the charges in place, make a run for the conveyor belt on the far wall and as you are doing so, bring up your detonator watch and blow the whole place to hell! Walk onto the conveyor to exit the level.

Level Guide - Mission 1.3

You begin this tiny level in the corridor which actually links in with the conveyor belt you climbed on to escape the chemical plant. First of all grab the hand grenades from the green crate and chuck one immediately into the doorway ahead. A guard is hiding inside and this will cause the whole area to explode; leaving the way clear for you to get the timed mines in this room. Now get on the conveyor again and walk outside. Shoot the guard on patrol and then enter the small building to your left. This is where the plane ignition key is kept.

Angle yourself near the door and peek around the corner

at the table where two guards are sitting with the key. Throw a hand grenade into the corner and stand back. Once the explosion has ripped through the room, nab the key and run around to the tank to the left side of the building. Climb aboard and drive towards the heavy gun emplacements. Stay on the left side of the runway, as this way only one gun can shoot at you.

If you are playing as an Agent, get in the plane pronto and escape. Secret Agents must fire the tank's gun at the missile launcher just before the plane. Aim at the top of the missile base, not the missiles themselves. OO Agents must then shoot the heavy gun turrets with the tank before getting in the plane. It all gets frantic near the end.

Mission 2: Severnaya
Level Guide -Mission 2.1

You start off in a small round clearing wearing your winter thermals. Time for action. Head round the path which bends to the left and pause by the empty watch towers and use your sniper rifle sights to survey the immediate area.

Carry on down the path and take out the lone guard walking towards you. Use the rifle to hit him right between the eyes! Before you reach the crossroads ahead, lean up against the left snow bank and look over to the right where there is a hut guarded by two guards. The most satisfying way to get rid of these guys is to shoot the barrels of toxic waste clustered around them. This will cause an almighty explosion and both will die. Inside the hut are two crates of grenade rounds for the launcher.

If playing on Agent level, you can now skip to the guide which explains powering down the satellite dish and escaping. Secret and OO Agents must accomplish a few extra tasks first.

The hut opposite this one is locked and it contains the key to the safe where the bunker plans are kept. You must get the key to this hut from a Siberian officer in a hut to the south. Get back on the main path heading south and watch

Nintendo 64 A-Z of Cheats Volume 2

out for another guard walking towards you. To your left is the old observatory which is a good vantage point for surveying the scene, but your shape will alert four or five snipers to the area, who can be easily picked off for extra ammo. Ahead of you is the faint shape of the satellite control building.

Take the next right turning and keep going straight past an empty hut on your right. To the left is the hut with the Siberian officer inside. The best way to get through this bit is to remember that glass is transparent, and thus if you position yourself correctly, you can take out the occupants of these huts from the outside; without them ever being alerted. This also works the other way, so shooting out of windows is a great way of clearing your path before going outside again.

Inside the hut is a white commando and the officer himself. Once you shoot out the glass, the officer will run out to attack you. Shoot him at close range, grab the large key, and then run inside to collect the awesome grenade launcher and to prepare for any snipers who have been alerted by the officer's gunfire.

Now return to the locked hut near the start of the level (by crossing the snow directly) and use the key to enter and get the safe key which is on the table.

Now that you have the key, you better head for the safe it opens, which is to the left of the satellite control building in the game. The safe is in the left building which is enclosed by fence. The path just outside is guarded by a sentry who can be shot from afar.

With plans safely tucked away in your furry jacket it's time to power down that comms dish. Head back up the path and you'll see the huge dish ahead of you. Enter through the door on the base and then climb up the stairs to a door straight ahead. Go through and you'll be in a room with a computer console in it. Simply press the B button to shut down the dish. If you blow this computer up, the mission will be a failure.

g   Now tool yourself up and prepare for enemy troops who will no doubt be alerted to your presence. All that remains for you to do is leg it out of the control building and head slightly to the left where the ventilation duct is waiting. Climb on top and then arm yourself with the silenced PP7 to shoot off the four padlocks before dropping into the next level.

Level Guide - Mission 2.2

You begin the mission on small gangway facing a door. Open it and immediately shoot the guard on the left who will set off the alarm if you let him. Now blast the other guy before he gets off too many shots. Look through the glass of the doors in this room and shoot out the first surveillance camera. Now go back across the gangway and peek around the corner to shoot the next camera. A guard will probably come through the door, and if he has a rounded hat then he will drop the computer room keycard. Cool.

Now go back through the room you've just cleared and step out into the corridor; killing any guards you encounter. One of them will have the general security keycard. The idea on this level is to be as quiet as possible. The guards can make as much noise as they want because their gunfire won't bring others to your position.

Sneak around to the other cameras in this top level and use your peek around corners move to shoot them without the alarm going off. There are approximately eight guards patrolling the corridors and a further five inside the rooms in this top section. The first objective won't be completed until you get the last surveillance camera on the lower level ,but you might as well clear the top level of troops first. Specifically, the computer room needs to be sanitised.

Head down the stairs and snipe-shoot the guard standing to the left of the entrance, and then watch out for one coming from the right. This is a large room dominated on the left wall by a huge video screen. This must be photographed by selecting the camera from the inventory and then standing directly in front of it.

The raised room to the right has three soldiers in it, including a brown shirt who has a PP7, and the other room opposite has the last surveillance camera which can be blasted by sneaking out from a corner and shooting the very front of it. Now you are free to photograph the main screen or go and talk to Boris the computer whiz who is standing over by the computer terminal in this room.

But first, grab the Goldeneye key from the table and use the key analyser to copy it. You must press the trigger twice – once to start the analyser going, and again to discard the real key.

Once contacted, traitor Boris will lead you slowly up to the computer room on the second level. If you have cleared this area before meeting Boris this will be a completely painless exercise as there are no more threats. The biggest problem would have been the three guards in the computer room, as a pitched gun battle with them is liable to leave those fragile mainframes completely pulverised!

Boris will walk over to the mainframe and begin typing. After a few seconds he will enter the password "Knockers" and this is a secret code to the elite guard to come and track you down. You had better watch the door from now on. Eventually, Boris will get into the computer and you are free to bring up the data thief in your inventory and then press the Z button to start downloading. Hopefully you will have time to do this before guards start arriving.

What many people don't realise is that the KF7 can be used – even on quiet missions – if you confine your shooting to single shots. It is particularly useful on this mission because PP7 ammo is scarce and you can easily run out of it in a tricky spot. In the computer room, for example, you can stand next to a pillar and pick off the so-called elite black guard using the KF7's zoom facility. They have to come through the door, so it's relatively straightforward to keep downing them as they rush to engage. You need to hit them in the head though, because they wear heavy body armour.

When you are ready, make your way down to to the exit, picking off guards as you go. Now make a run for the last corridor, which has two green guards waiting at the end. Open the steel door and exit the level.

Mission 3.1: Kirghizstan
Level Guide Mission 3.1

From the first missile tube, open the door and shoot the two guards on duty here. You can start with the silenced PP7, but remember that the KF7 needs to be used in sort bursts, or more guards will be alerted.

If you're playing on the OO Agent difficulty level, the plastique charges will already be primed and you'll have just eight minutes to complete the whole thing. Secret Agents have even less time – seven and a half minutes Cripes!

Up the stairs the corridor bends left and there are three guards standing behind a steel crate. They may be alerted by initial gunfire. Use your crafty sneak-peek move to take out the guards with minimum fuss (head shots to conserve ammo of course). The door at the end leads to the first fuel room. There is a solitary guard hiding behind a buttress to the right, but there are also innocent scientists. Shoot near the guy in white on the far left and he will drop a security keycard. There are two pieces of satellite circuitry on the table here. If on OO Agent level, plant your plastique in the red light area between toxic symbols on the right wall.

With the keycard you can now open the security door at the top of the stairs. Behind it is a long corridor with a T junction. Two guards patrol here and can be shot from afar if you're accurate enough with the PP7. Take the right turn (the left leads to a dead-end silo) and make a note to turn right at every opportunity until you get to the last silo.

Kill the lone guard in the silo and then go through the next door to face two more sleeping guards in the long corridor. At the top of the stairs and around the left bend there are some explosive barrels and two more guards down the end, hiding behind bullet-proof steel boxes. You must be quick to

Nintendo 64 A-Z of Cheats Volume 2

take these guys out or a stray bullet could easily turn your hiding place into a raging inferno! The next door leads to the second fuel room.

Immediately inside the door to the right are two guards: one right next to you, the other in the distance. Dispatch both with extreme prejudice. Frighten the scientists to get the key security keycard and computer circuitry. If you are on OO Agent, plant your next piece of plastique and head for the door at the top of the stairs. One guard stands right next to the door (head shot) and three others patrol the next T junction. Switch to your KF7 and use the zoom function to pick them off while leaning in from the frame of the door. A sneaky guard waits for you behind a steel crate on the left side of the junction. Once dispatched, head right to the next silo.

Two dim-witted guards stand on the gangway – kill them both and run straight through to the next room. This is full of guards, three of whom are right next to the door, so you'll have your work cut out for you dodging bullets while on a thin platform. Head up the stairs and bend left. The next fuel room has two guards in it, plus a cluster of scientists who give up the usual circuitry and keycard.

You should now have all the telemetric data to complete Objective three, and all the circuitry for Objective four. All that's left is to photograph the satellite and get the hell out of there. If playing on OO Agent, plant the next piece of plastique here and then move on as the clock has almost run out.

There is another T-junction ahead, with two guards stationed at the end, one behind a steel box. Another couple of back-up men lurk on the junction itself. If you are playing on the Agent level, a turn left here and through into the silo will reveal one guard and some body armour. This is sadly missing for both other difficulty levels.

Turn right at the T-junction though and it's through another gangway with two guards standing at the far end. Use your sneak attack to blast them both, or you can even use your KF7 to zoom right in and get them both with head shots. The next short corridor has a series of steel boxes zig-zagged across the path to provide cover for three armed and alert guards. You must snipe these guys quick, or you'll be hit many times in this ambush. And once you've dealt with them, there's another cluster of men just around the left corner.

The final fuel room has the Goldeneye satellite (see left) in it and this must be photographed using your spy camera used last in the bunker. There are a couple of troops in this room, and some might even try to walk up to the top section to alert the men there. Shoot him in the back if he tries this.

Now that you have completed all the assignments (OO Agents should place the last charge in this room), you must exit the room (you do not need a keycard) and face a squad of troops headed by General Ourumov himself. Use your side-snipe move to take out some offenders, then charge the rest; zig-zagging up the corridor – if you're quick, you might even be able to get Ourumov's briefcase!

Chase Ourumov through the corridors to the end of the game (first left, then into two final computer rooms. The exit to the level is an elevator, but be careful not to get caught in the first computer room when a stray bullet sends the whole place up. The chain reaction means nothing can survive in there.

Mission 4.1: Monte Carlo
Level Guide Mission 4.1

From the speedboat, climb up the gangplank and head towards the back of the ship. You will come to two sets of steps: one forward, one aft. Take the aft set, as the other one leads to the bridge and it is very difficult to save the hostage from this direction. Open the door and immediately move to the left of the corridor to avoid eye contact with the first terrorist. Now pop up and shoot him with your silenced D5K. The next door is on your right. Stand in the centre and open it with your gun sight ready on the room. As soon as it opens, blast the left terrorist as he is the one who will execute the hostage inside. Pull back out of the room and wait for the other terrorist to come forward where you can shoot him.

Now move into the room and quickly turn 90° right and shoot the distance terrorist in the next room, as he is about to shoot a hostage. enter the second room; taking out terrorists appearing from the left. Be careful of getting too close to the computer consoles, as they will explode; taking you with them.

Head out into the corridor in front of you and scout left and right for terrorists on patrol. There should be one on either side, but the right route will bring reinforcements from down below if you give them enough time. Follow the bodies down the first set of stairs down and to the right.

The route bears right and there's a dumb guard standing in the darkness. Practice your marksmanship skills by shooting him through the skull. Ignore the door on the right, but move past it swiftly to avoid taking on the guards just yet. There will be a set of stairs going down on your right, and a guard at the bottom. Shoot both him and the one on your level before moving around the stairs and shooting the guard in the room full of boxes to the right. You can now descend into the ship even further.

There's another terrorist near the bottom of the stairs and you will also see the engine room door on the right, with an accompanying roaring sound. You won't be taking this way into the bridge, as it offers few vantage points. Instead, walk around to the left and through the door.

As it swings open you can see a hostage quivering in front of a gun. Swing into the small room and shoot the terrorist on the right first, and try to keep moving so that the other one won't hit you. Follow the corridor around until you reach an open doorway. You can see the back of a terrorist who is about to pepper a hostage with lead, so quickly shoot him (in the back, OO7 I am ashamed of you!)

g and watch out because the fleeing hostage will open the next door and the terrorists inside will start shooting if you're in their line of fire.

There are three blokes in this corridor and to the right is staircase H leading up to the helicopter hanger. Ahead is the other entrance to the engine room. This is the one you're going to enter. The engine room is a large chamber set on two levels.

If you haven't already alerted them, there should be a guard to your far left, one in front of you (some distance away) and then three on the bottom level. Silently shoot the top ones, and then if playing on Secret Agent level, run over to the computer console directly in front of you and use the defuser to make the engine room bomb safe. Walk over to the door where you entered and stand on the edge of the walkway. Point your gun downwards and you should be able to shoot the terrorist hiding below without him even seeing you. Walk down the steps and head up past the engine itself. When the engine casing becomes thinner you should be able to see a hostage and a terrorist to the left of you. Take the bad guy out before he knows what's going on, and then surprise the guy hiding to the right with a few short bursts from your D5K.

Leave the engine room using the door you entered with and head up staircase H on the left. This will lead you up to a short passage guarded by two sleepy terrorists and if you continue onwards you will reach a large shutter with the Pirate helicopter beyond; ready to take off. Select the tracker bug and use your gun sights to aim it on the fuselage. Objective four will be completed.

Walk off the helicopter pad on the port (left) side of the ship and head along the outside of the ship up staircase E, down C and up A (see page 52). You can now enter the bridge via the set of steps in front of you. The moment you open the door to the bridge you must get a bead on the terrorist who is about to execute the hostage. Take him and the other two out, then walk over to the bomb on the

Nintendo 64 A-Z of Cheats Volume 2

computer console and use the defuser to make it safe.

By now the last hostage will have reached safety and Objective one will be complete. You can now use the other door to the bridge and make your way to the waiting speedboat to complete the mission.

Mission 5: Severnaya
Level Guide Mission 5.1

Just you and your trusty PP7, James, and it's back to Severnaya for a second helping of the snow level. The idea is to seal off the area from anyone escaping and then attack the bunker direct. You begin in the same circular clearing, but this time the sky is dark red and there are more troops wandering around the complex. Head off down the path and you may come across three or more snow troopers using Klobbs. Dispatch them and head on past the two crossroads up ahead.

This time the two huts to the left and right are empty, so ignore them and head on where you'll come to a split in the path. Take the right route and head up to the hut where you encountered the Siberian Officer in the last snow mission. Approach this far hut from behind and walk right up to the sides. There is a video camera attached to the front of the hut. Use your sneak-peek move to shoot off the camera and stop the alarm from being raised.

If you stand right up against the first window to the right of the camera you should be able to see the Officer standing inside. With careful aiming, you can easily shoot him in the head through the glass and then rush in to grab the comms key. If the heat is on, why not close the door and pick off approaching guards through the windows before moving on.

Leave the hut, turn left and run straight out over the snow dunes to avoid any troops on the paths. Security patrols will now be increased, so there is a greater chance of coming across a few squads on your way to the next objective. Head down to the huge communications building in the middle of the levl and use the comms key to open the double front doors. Run through and up the first set of steps; pausing to turn 90° left and scan the wall for the tell-tale video camera which would set off the alarm if you carried on running.

Pick off the camera from this distance using an extremely accurate PP7, or if you have nabbed a KF7, use the zoom function to take it out first time. Remember though, short bursts only on the machine gun, or the whole Russian army will come looking for you.

Follow the walkway around and go through the door directly in front of you. This is the communications room. Switch to a machine gun and blast the computers to bits. First of all it will say they're damaged, then if you persist, they will be destroyed. Watch out here because guards will try to enter the room from both doors as you concentrate on completing this objective. As soon as you hear a door being opened, stop what you are doing and cover your back. This is where sound is so important in Goldeneye.

Fight your way out of the comms building (use the right door from the comms room and you will be outside. You can now briefly spot any approaching troops and perhaps even pick them off from afar.

Now, if playing on OO Agent level you must head down from the comms building to shoot out the two remaining surveillance cameras located in two building complexes. Watch out for troops as you do this, particularly on the last one, as the hut where the camera is located is full of armoured guards having a tea break. All the huts in this area hold nothing of value, so don't bother entering them, not unless you need them to cover from patrols. In fact, be wary of the last hut which faces the one with the camera on it. Inside is a model of the helicopter you are about to destroy, but if it gets shot, the whole hut goes up. Obviously some kind of trap for people messing about with this guy's models.

For the final objective (or two if you're playing on Secret

Agent or above) leg it around to the helicopter landing pad and fire the timed mine onto the chopper as it prepares to take off. Take cover in the shelter of the bunker and watch the helicopter burn before turning and entering the bunker to complete the mission. Unfortunately this means you are then captured, and must start the next level in the jail. There is no way to prevent this from happening.

Level Guide Mission 5.2
Oh the humanity! Bond has been taken prisoner and dumped in one of the deepest cells. The idea is to escape and infiltrate the installation from within, and there are plenty of sub-tasks to complete; depending on which difficulty you are playing.

First of all, have a chat with Natalya in the neighbouring cell, but don't let her out until you have cleared most of the level. Now go over to the front of your cell and activate your watch magnet near the rather obvious cell key. Hey presto! The cell key will come into your possession. Now switch to hand-to-hand combat (bet you never thought you'd be this desperate, OO7!) and wait until the guard is right by your cell before opening the door and karate-chopping his neck. You will now get a KF7, the key for Natalya's cell and if you're lucky, during the struggle you'll get some throwing knives too, although these do not always appear (a bug perhaps?)

Walk over to the main doors at the end of the corridor (forget Natalya for now) and switch to your KF7. "What's this?" You must be thinking. "Surely the noise from the gun will alert all of the guards?" Well yes and no. If you simply fire the machine gun willy nilly, then hundreds of guards will overwhelm you. But if you use the zoom facility and tap the Z button for a single shot, you can shoot many of the guards in the head and no more will come. This sneaky tactic was discovered after many failed attempts to use the frankly useless throwing knives. These may be deadly, but they are hopelessly inaccurate and you have to keep picking them up.

g

Shoot the first guard who appears through the head and then go through the doors and prepare to clear the corridor on the left, and the room ahead and left. If guards try to rush you, run back to behind another door and prepare to fire using the zoom again. The door ahead of you is locked and will only be opened by a guard if you make a lot of noise. Sometimes though, he will go on patrol and walk around, so you can get him then.

With the immediate area clear, head down the left path and up the stairs. There will be three or four guards patrolling here, one of them holds keycard A which opens the locked door near the cells. Use your sneaky round corners shot to take them out and then turn right and right again into the room. This room has two guards in it, plus the staff list needed if you're playing on Secret Agent level or above. If you can get through the first locked door near the cells, then you are able to approach the guard with the casualty list a lot easier. for the rest of you mortals, here's how to get there unscathed.

Head out of the room with the staff lists and turn right. Go up the next set of closed doors and wait for a guard to appear. Shoot him through the glass and carry on through to a T junction. Check each direction quickly and shoot any guards here. Now edge around the right wall and use your zoom to shoot out the first surveillance camera which is down the hall on the left. There is no need to go left here as it leads to drone guns, although there is a set of body armour if playing on Agent level only.

Turn right and sneak down the corridor a little way until you come to a door on the left and one on the right. Open the right door, but stay pressed right because there is a camera right inside. Shoot this and then enter the room with the small generator in it. There is a door to the left, but approach with caution. Immediately above the door is a camera. Walk through a little way, look up and blast it before going on. This is one that always gets missed.

A guard has his back to you in the next room. Shoot him ruthlessly in the head and get the CCTV tape from the table. Objective two will now be completed. Shoot any guards from the windows and then go out through the door and turn right, then left down the stairs. At the bottom will be two guards standing sentry: one on the left, one on the right. Be careful here, as there is a surveillance camera on the facing wall to the left. This must be destroyed or the alarm will go off. Turning left or right here will lead you round to a large room containing a set of body armour (for Agents only) and the casualty list if the guard hasn't wandered too far.

Leave this area by the steps and head up to the corridor to a T Junction. There should be a set of stairs going down to your right and another corridor to the left. If playing on Secret Agent or OO Agent, go left and open the first set of doors on your right. Walk up to the next set of doors, shoot the guard through the glass and slink into the room via the left wall. Take out the camera and get the gold key that was dropped by the guard.

This key (and one held by a guard in the safe room itself) opens the safe in the room near the cells. Inside is the Goldeneye operations manual and a silenced PP7. Objective four will now be completed if playing on OO Agent level.

You can now go and get Natalya and lead her to the stairs, or clear out the last area first. At the bottom of the stairs is the large control room where you took pictures last time. The layout has not changed. As you round the corner you will spot two guards on the raised platform, and two more standing to attention by the exit doors. Cap these guys first at long range. and then turn right and shoot the two guys on the raised platform here. There is a third guard in the alcove. Now move around the room; hugging the left wall to the next raised platform fronted by glass. Shoot the camera here and if you have Natalya then exit through the glass doors, or if not, go and get her!

Mission 6: St Petersburg
Level Guide Mission 6.1

Bond starts the level near the sickle monument and not far from the main gate. Russian troops will begin approaching from all angles, so immediately head for the two tall white pillars and then this will lead down a slope. Watch out for guards at the bottom of the incline – you may have to angle your gun sight to shoot them from above. The best tactic here is to keep running past the many broken monuments (stay left if you can as this offers the most direct route) and shoot guards only if they are in your way. If you stay to engage them all, you'll be quickly surrounded.

Stay pressed up against the left of the park and you'll soon round a bend (over a small hill with railings to the right and three pillars) and see the distinctive red container that Valentin is waiting in. Check to see if the coast is clear and go in and chat to the ex-KGB man for what seems like hours (he's such a bore). Valentin will explain that Janus is a Lienz Cosak and that he cannot be trusted and then depart; having set-up the meeting. When he has finished his speech, Objective one will be completed.

Leave the container and turn left. Again, hug the left wall of the park until you see a mock tank and a hammer & sickle statue which you should head towards and past. The park will now bend to the right, but you should remain hugging the left wall. Strangely there are no more government troops around...

You will soon come to a mass of broken concrete. Head in and you'll see a giant statue of a hand with some body armour lying in front of it. This appears on all difficulty levels. Work your way out of this mini maze and carry on into the park towards the now-visible statue of Lenin on the hill.

As you reach the statue, the Janus group will slowly appear from the shadows led by their leader – none other than OO6, Alec Trevelyan! You must have your gun put away for this conversation or the meeting will be instantly

Nintendo 64 A-Z of Cheats Volume 2

cancelled and the group will open fire with their automatic shotguns. When Alec's speech about his hard done-by parents and the British government is over, he will announce that Natalya is by the Pirate helicopter at the park gates and that there is a bomb rigged to go off in three minutes – suddenly you have a deadline!

Rush the Janus troops and simultaneously arm yourself; trying to take out one or two of the black clad thugs as you run. Head straight out of the park preferably down the right side of the park; reversing the way you came in. Alec's thugs will try to hunt you down, but if you kill one of them, you get the highly effective automatic shotgun which wastes most guards in a single shot.

Trevelyan's men will try to cut you off at every turn, so waste no time and shoot anything that moves. As the clock ticks down, you should be heading to the start of the level and up the hill with Trevelyan's thugs not far behind. Luckily for you, they desist their attack as you near the Pirate helicopter.

At the top of the hill you will start to hear the rotor blades of the Pirate helicopter and Objective three will be completed. However, as you run up to the unconscious Natalya who is lying right next to the chopper, a proximity mine with a timed fuse of just 15 seconds kicks in, so you must wake her up – quick. Luckily this is not that difficult and having explained the situation to her, Natalya will follow Bond wherever he goes with eight seconds still to spare. Get safely out of the way and watch the Pirate helicopter explode.

Now you must find the helicopter's flight recorder which has been blown clear of the wreckage. Head back down the hill and search the immediate area for the bright orange box. It is never in the same place twice, so you'll just have to do some donkey work. Remember that Trevelyan's men are still out there. When you get back to Natalya, Mishkin has already taken her prisoner. Open the gates to end the mission.

Level Guide Mission 6.2

You begin by being interrogated by two thugs in a small locked room. First order of the day is getting back your PP7, which is handily lying on the table in front of you. It's almost as if they're daring you to go for yer guns! You can either walk up and grab your weapons, or use your watch magnet – it doesn't really matter, although if you use the latter, you can already be standing ready to shoot the first guard.

One item of interest is that if you start shooting willy nilly, hundreds of Russians will pour into the cell from the adjoining rooms. Instead, use only single shots to the head in this room, recover the door key and then go out into the corridor. Open the facing door, and leg it into the larger room beyond.

This next room has a couple of sleepy guards in it, but more importantly, a piece of body armour in the middle. Grab this and head straight on through; turning right at the end, and then right again up a set of steps and through a door. You are now at a crossroads with a guard straight ahead in the distance, and one to the left and right.

From our experience you should shoot the one ahead, turn right and blast this guy before he knows what's going on. You can now duck into one of the rooms on the right, and then turn and shoot down the corridor at the brace of guards now appearing in the distance. Note that there are boxes stacked up against the left wall, and these can be shot to cause damage to the advancing guards. A machine gun battle will now take place, with up to ten guards charging your position. Keep shooting wildly, but when leaning out of the room, make sure you don't get caught by the explosion from the boxes stacked behind you.

With a pile of rapidly dissolving bodies in the doorway, you should now be left alone and the rest of the guards in the complex will go about their business. Use this as a cue to turn right out of the room and press the B button at the wall where the pile of boxes stood. This is a secret passage that leads left to a small room with three DD44-toting guards. Wipe out all traces of life from this room and then exit via the door to the left. Now head straight up the corridor and open the door at the far end. Kill any guards in your way, including the one hiding behind the three bookcases here.

Take out any alerted guards and head around the balcony to the staircase. If playing on Secret Agent or above, read on, if on Agent, skip to the end where you rescue Natalya.

Go down the stairs and through the door on the right. You are now in another area of the archives covered in shelves. Head left and along the wall until you come to a bend to the left in the room and a door in front of you. Open the door and go through to the end of the resultant corridor. The door on the right leads to a small courtyard. Waste all guards in this area. Now go back along the corridor with the light shining through and enter the door on the right. Make sure there are no guards hanging around or they'll cause trouble in this room. Defence Minister Mishkin is inside, but the room is packed with explosives and one rogue shot from a stray guard could destroy the lot!

Talk to Mishkin and he'll give you the key to the safe behind him. Inside is the Pirate flight recorder needed to complete Objective three if playing on Secret Agent or above. Now go back up to the top of the staircase. Go through the door here. There will be three guards in this bookcase area and on the far wall, a large angled door, with a single one to the right of it.

Enter the single door to find Natalya being interrogated. Shoot the two guards (watch out for the fleeing woman), and then try and catch Natalya up. Once found, lead her over to the large windows. All that's left is to shoot out the glass and jump through with Natalya in tow to complete the mission successfully.

Mission 6.3: St Petersburg
Level Guide Mission 6.3

The fun begins in an alley outside the archives. Walk forward until you see an open gate on the left. Use your sneak-peek move to lean out and pick off the two guards standing in the distance. Your gun shots will alert more guards – four or five in total – and as soon as the coast is clear, run forward to the fence and check for any more.

With the area cleared, turn right and go through the next open gate. To your immediate right is another guard. Shoot him by leaning around the corner and then turn left and head down the small alley that runs parallel to the tank. Around the second bend is a guard, and then some more on each subsequent 90° turn. Up on the left is a doorway leading to a talk with Valentin who will then add six minutes to your mission time. What a helpful chap! You must have at least 45-60 seconds on the clock when you meet Valentin, as this is how long he takes to phone his operatives and get the time extended. After speaking to him, turn left out of the building and run over to where two guards are shooting from open windows. Walk right through the right window and you're in a room with a guard and a set of body armour. A hole in the wall to the left leads to another guard and a grenade launcher with some ammo.

Now you must run back to the tank and use it to drive around the streets to the exit. When you come to a minefield, use your tank gun or grenades to clear it, and while driving, use your KF7 to shoot troops, or run them over. Many of the troops on the street have rocket launchers, and they can be identified by a high pitched whine when it is launched. Concentrate on them first and you should make it through this mission.

Nintendo 64 A-Z of Cheats Volume 2

Mission 6.4: St Petersburg
Level Guide Mission 6.4

Entering through an alley at the side of the depot, you first head forward and then turn right. There is a warehouse shutter door on your right, but more importantly, the first armed guard is hidden by a container to the left. Remember, 007, that all the guards in the Janus depot have body armour and must therefore be shot in the head to get rid of them quickly. Otherwise you can waste up to five bullets putting one down.

To the right of the first warehouse are a couple of guards standing to attention among the containers. Wipe these out with as few shots as possible, so as not to alert too many others to your position so early on. There is some body armour in the bottom corner here, behind the container if you are playing on the Agent level only. Otherwise it is gone.

Head up and turn right into the first warehouse for a piece of body armour if playing on Secret Agent level. Now move to the steel gate midway through the first section. There will be armed guards all around, so take them out with the minimum of fuss. You will now have almost certainly picked up two D5Ks and can therefore double your firepower. It is also worth mentioning that if you come across iron railings or wire, the guards treat this as a solid wall, but you can still shoot through it.

At the T junction, turn left and fight your way to the shutter door in the far left corner. This is the computer network building. Enemy guards are all around, so quickly open the door and dart in; shooting the two sentries to the left and right. Do not get knocked to the extremities of this room as there is a large rapid-firing drone gun in the top left corner that will make mincemeat out of you! There are about five guards in this room.

g Now that you are in the computer building, close the shutter door and edge over to the far left of the steel crates where you came in. The drone gun is the major obstacle here. Instead of trying to sneakily get a shot in, the best way to destroy it is to point your gun up to roughly the right height, and then strafe in and out; getting in a few hits each time. Drone guns are not meant to withstand damage, so it will explode after only a few hits.

You can now enter the main room, but keep listening for the sound of the shutter door opening, as this indicates more troops are on the way. There is also one more guard craftily waiting between the two mainframes. Don't get shot in the back will you, 007?

With the computer room cleared of danger, walk over to the desk on the left, nearest the large video screen, and pick up the safe key. Objective three will now be completed. All that remains for you to do here is shoot both mainframes (tall-ish green computer things at the back) and then the large video wall showing a map of the world. Objective two is now complete. Leave through the only door, being wary to avoid troops who may have massed outside preparing to ambush you.

Your next target (if playing on OO Agent level) is the illegal arms cache and it is to be found in the second warehouse on the right as you exit the computer network building. There are no sentry guards, but there are three of them inside among the boxes of arms, so be careful where you shoot those bullets. The best way to clear this room is to shoot the nearest guy, then run up the stairs to the raised platform at the back of the room where you can pick off the other two at will. This room is an Aladin's cave for Bond, because you can stock up on rocket launchers, KF7s and proximity mines before torching the place. When you leave, you should be a right Rambo!

Now on to the safe where the blueprints are kept. You will need to head straight up from the arms cache and then to the left as you reach the very top. There are two bits of

Nintendo 64 A-Z of Cheats Volume 2

body armour on the way up for both Agents and Secret Agents, and as you pass the train on your right, you should see a door down a small ramp up ahead. Enter here. The house is empty (how careless of Janus), so run up the stairs, bear left and open the safe to recover the blueprints and complete Objective four (if playing as Secret Agent). Now go through the door on the right. This leads you to a spacious warehouse. Open the shutters on one wall to find the train. Finally, shoot the two guards and enter the train to complete the mission.

Mission 6.5: St Petersburg
Level Guide Mission 6.5

Start off by walking up to the stacked up crates and shooting the only guard visible, who is standing to your diagonal left. Watch out for shots hitting the crates next to you though; causing them to explode. Now push yourself up against the right wall and shoot the guard who is way off in the distance but can just be seen next to the two crates piled on top of each other. You can now move further forward and, using your strafing move to duck out from behind the crates, shoot a few shots into the darkness, then get back behind cover. Keep doing this until nothing shoots back, then proceed.

The first brake unit is at the end of the carriage. Shoot it until it explodes and then arm yourself with one of the fallen D5Ks. Stand to the right of the door at the end and open both it and the inner one as well. There are three guards who immediately fire on you in this next carriage. The closest is standing to the left. As you open the door, let him have it with the machine gun before retreating to avoid injury.

Pick off the other two by popping into the doorway, letting loose a few shots, and then retreating. When the immediate area is clear, move forwards; ducking in and out of the crates for cover. You will come to some steel crates. This is the halfway point and there are loads of guards on

g the other side. You usually get a couple of black elite guards here, so try pressing the right shoulder button and the down yellow button to crouch, and then walk around the crates to take the men by surprise. You might also be able to shoot a few using the steel crate as cover because it won't explode.

When all are dead, move up the carriage and shoot out the second brake unit. Watch out though, because sometimes one of the guards from the next compartment will open the door ahead of you and open fire.

The next carriage is divided into a corridor and ten compartments, with a toilet at either end. There are softer guards in the corridor, and these can be pulped with little or no fuss. As you do so though, make sure you check the first locked toilet, as this contains a sneaky guard who will only come out and attack once you've passed him.

Fight your way up the carriage (these ones are much easier) and shoot out the third brake unit at the end. As before, the guards in the next compartment often get bored and open the door prematurely. Punish them with hot lead and don't stop shooting unless a) you're dead, b) they're dead, c) someone kicks the power lead out of the N64.

The next carriage is the reverse of the one before, with the sleepers located on the right side. The fourth brake unit is located to the left at the start, so don't miss it, or you'll have to come all the way back here. Apart from the men in the corridor, there are two guards hiding in the second compartment along, and they will come out when you pass them and try to shoot you in the back. Kill them before they get the chance. Down the corridor there are three more guards holding the door.

Behind the next set of double doors is a black elite commando with body armour, but luckily the D5Ks seem to just eat through this protective material. The decor is now a fetching shade of green by the way. The next room has another commando standing in a straight line down the carriage and is easily picked off (not very Elite are they?).

Nintendo 64 A-Z of Cheats Volume 2

More black guards occupy the two toilets in the annex, and then two more hold sway in the next larger room. You should be able to get another D5K out of one of them.

The black guard in the next corridor has his back to you at first (more fool him), and once you've blasted the fifth brake unit, another black guard appears mysteriously behind you, so stay sharp and get some cover quick!

Now you're through to the final carriage which is decked out in white and has just one guard waiting in the corridor. Blast him and then shoot the sixth and final brake unit which is located right by the door. The brakes will screech and gradually the train comes to a halt. Perplexed by the lack of motion, two black elite guards storm into the white carriage from the front and both of these bad boys carry two D5Ks. Silence them forever and grab the train door key from one of them. Cheers mate!

The rest of the objectives for the level all take place in the final room. Trevelyan and Onatopp are right at the back of the carriage and General Ourumov is holding Natalya at gunpoint. They invite you in, which means you can take your time aiming your crosshair at Ourumov's head. You can also try to shoot Onatopp too and this gives you bags of extra time. Whatever happens, a large bullet proof shield cuts you off from them and a bomb is primed to destroy the train. Natalya will make busy with the computer to discover the whereabouts of Janus' base (Objective three) and if playing on OO Agent, crack Boris's password.

You must use your laser watch to blast the metal strips off the hatch on the floor of the compartment. Stand near it, face down, and use the crosshair to aim the watch exactly. With a steady hand you should be through with 30 seconds to spare. Once Natalya has the location (Cuba), you must jump down the hole, turn right and keep running as the train explodes. If you get out with enough time, the mission will end when you clear the front of the train. Try to zig-zag as you run because Janus' troops are shooting at you from behind.

Mission 7: Cuba
Level Guide Mission 7.1

Beautiful Natalya joins you in this mission and she is pretty damn handy with that gun of hers. As the plane you arrived in explodes, enemy troops are drawn by the noise. Initially, two men will approach, but you needn't bother using your trusty PP7 because Natalya will nail them both before you can say "vodka martini." Walk over to where the men where felled and grab their AR33 assault rifles. This is a fantastically powerful weapon which not only delivers hundreds of high velocity rounds a minute, but also give you a long zoom facility – perfect for cutting through the murk of the jungle environment.

Head out into the pea souper; nipping from tree to tree and using everything for cover in case you are suddenly faced with a squad of troops. Use the zoom to search the jungle ahead before moving on. Natalya will follow out in the open, and it is important to keep from being harmed. You will come across several troops in the first stretch of jungle and then a drone gun right out in the open. Hide behind the thickest tree and then gradually move out until you can just see a corner of the gun. Let loose with your AR33 and you can take out the drone without putting yourself at risk.

Make sure you grab the body armour in the top left corner of this glade, and remember to pick up all the ammo dropped by your foes. Head around to the right, with you and Natalya taking care of the next squad of men who advance on your position as soon as they spot you. At the end of the next section the path bends to the left and there's another drone gun defended by three guards. Sharp eyed Bonds will also notice a piece of body armour near the far wall under a fern.

With Natalya unharmed, sneak through the undergrowth further into the jungle. Another drone gun awaits, and guess what? More camouflaged troops. You will also come across a large wooden watch tower, but this is just scenery and no-one is ready to take pot shots at you from it. More body armour can be found at the top here just before the path bends to the right. The armour is for Agents and Secret Agents only though.

The jungle soon peters out and you'll come to a bridge. Prepare for your confrontation with Xenia Onatopp! Walk halfway across the bridge and when her message comes on the screen, pull back and drop a mine near the end of the bridge. Now stand to the left or right of the rope bridge and prepare to detonate the mine when Xenia reaches it. Boom! But she isn't killed outright and you must finish her off with the AR33. One important tip is that Xenia will not fire on you if you are not directly in front of her. This means that you can get a good few hits in while she is crossing the bridge and she will not be able to retaliate.

With Xenia dead you can grab her rocket launcher and RCP-90 machine gun, which is perfect for taking out the ammo dump at the end of the game (if playing on Secret Agent level). When you cross the bridge, watch out for the drone gun which is to your left. This is facing forwards, so you don't usually find out about it until it blasts you in the back!

The jungle bends around to the right, but take this section cautiously, as there are two troopers in the cave to your right, plus a drone gun straight ahead. Use Xenia's rocket launcher to take out the drone gun (and guards if you want), and spray the area with your AR33 just to be sure. If the cave has been cleared properly, head into it and through the tunnel ahead to a wide open cave. There are two guards here: one on the right, and one on the left. You should also be able to see the ladder ahead of you. This is the route you are going to take because it cuts out a lot of guards and takes you directly to the arms dump.

Before you climb the ladder, check the passage to the right and shoot anyone who tries to interfere. If you're lucky, one of the charging troops will be stacked with grenades, and the whole lot will go up; giving you more time than usual. Now climb the ladder, but before you reach the

g top, just look over the lip of the cliff face and use your RCP-90 to blast the drone gun pointing right at you. Now climb up and shoot the final gun to the right. You are now in the ammo dump. Plant some remote mines and then head round to the right; ignoring the troops hiding behind steel crates ahead of you.

Detonate the explosives, and hopefully Natalya will now join you from going the long route. Killing those troops below will have helped her chances. To complete the level, you must get past the guards ahead and then run through a small passage to a lift. To do this without getting a scratch, fire a salvo of grenades into the crates area and then charge them with the RCP-90. This rapid firing machine gun will slaughter any remaining guards and you should then run to the exit before more guards regenerate.

Mission 7.2: Cuba
Level Guide Mission 7.2

Agents will have a simple start to this level, with only some guards to take out in the initial room. Secret Agents and above, however, have a much harder job because drone guns are placed at three points in the room, and must be taken out with pinpoint accuracy and no loss of energy.

First of all run straight out of the lift (the first drone gun fires, but misses you if you keep moving up to the wall) and shoot the guard to the left with your PP7. Now run back into the lift, turn and shoot the guards as they come into view directly in front. This is so that you don't have to run the gauntlet to pick up their dropped D5Ks. Switch to the machine gun and shoot the first drone gun. This is to the right of the lift entrance. You only need to see a tiny bit of the drone gun to destroy it, so don't go taking any chances, and if you accidentally fall into its range, move quickly into a safe spot. These babies take a lot of energy!

Now press up to the wall to the left of the lift entrance and edge forward until you can nab the second drone gun. Use the gun's muzzle flash to see where to hit it. With that

Nintendo 64 A-Z of Cheats Volume 2

destroyed, move into the open and turn slightly right to shoot the blind side of the gun right up in the roof. To clear the room, attract the attention of the three guards and then shoot them as they approach. Pick up all that lovely ammo and then go and get Natalya. If you didn't get hit at all, she will say "James, you were wonderful." Cheers luv. She will now start accessing the computer terminal.

After a minute or so, Natalya will get the blast door furthest from her open and this is how you get into the Janus complex. At the end of the corridor is a small ramp and a tiny room with two guards in it. You should be able to take out at least one of them from the door. Now run down the corridor and watch out for the opening to the right near the ramp, as this is full of guards who will shoot on sight. You might try providing covering fire to stun them before diving for the small room. Kill the last man here and then get the box of remote mines and the ammo. Now you are ready to get all those troops.

Edge up the ramp and use your strafe buttons to move out into the corridor and spray the area with lead. Luckily for you, some of the men here have hand grenades, but haven't got a clue how to use them. More often than not, they will throw them short as soon as you appear, so if you duck back into the small room you will hear the explosions and the guards all dying. Now mop up the rest of the men, especially the white-haired one at the front. You might want to try a remote mine for good measure.

Once past the steel boxes here, get their ammo and head into the small passage. There is a room with a large generator in it, and four guards. Shoot these from the passage and move up the steps to the security door. Open this while standing to the right and shoot the dozy guy standing on the left before he knows what's happening. Now wait for two others to appear at the door and then take out the remaining one standing at the bottom of the stairs through the door. You are now entering the main control room.

g

Through the blast door is Boris mucking about on his computers. Approach him and he will start making excuses before trying to pull a gun. If you are standing right next to him you will automatically take the gun off him and he'll run off in horror. Don't shoot him, or Natalya will not help you. The best tactic now is to get protection, so follow Boris up two flights of stairs to the top level and over to the left where you'll crouch down and enter a small chamber with the only piece of body armour on the level.

Now go down a level and kill the two men standing to the left and right of the stairs. The central area is now clear of men. Go to the blast door opposite to the one you entered through. Behind this door are three guards and a long room with two drone guns facing you and two to the left and right. Step back from the open door and shoot the guards as they come to attack you. Now stand well back from the open door and face it directly. The drone guns work on range, so if you're far enough away, they won't fire and you can pick them off at will. Unfortunately, there is no easy way to take the two right near the entrance, because if you try to get one, the other will shoot you in the back. You should be able to just get a corner of one in your sights though, or you could try throwing a remote mine near one.

Inside this room is one of the armoured mainframes, so why not plant a remote mine on it so that you don't have to enter this room again?

Now is a good time to take out the two accessible mainframes on the bottom level (near where you first found Boris) and the two on the middle floor also. This should leave just one mainframe which is located behind a locked door on the bottom level. The reason for working on this Objective before getting Natalya is because once she has escaped, the guards will still keep coming and it means you only have one mainframe to destroy instead of six.

With the area cleared you should now head up to the second level, around the main video screen room and through the blast door. This will lead you to Natalya who is

Nintendo 64 A-Z of Cheats Volume 2

waiting to come in and get on that Goldeneye computer.

Natalya will run to the central computer in the room with the large video screen and begin typing. After a few seconds, she will set of an alarm and guards will begin pouring into the complex from the balconies, stairs and behind the two plates of glass directly to the left and right of Natalya. Your job is to keep moving and blast all of these troops before they can stop Natalya from completing her task. This is an incredibly hard task and you must find out which troops are going for Natalya directly, and which ones are just trying to get your attention. From exhaustive study, we have ascertained that the soldiers with white hair (and no hats) are the ones who mainly target Natalya, whereas the others try to draw your fire.

After a long gun battle, Natalya will alter the satellite's trajectory and Objective two will be completed. You must then escort her to the blast door where she came in and then to the lift. Objective One will now be completed. Now fight your way down to the bottom level (more troops will arrive to block your way) and enter the right blast door which was previously locked. Inside are two guards and the last armoured mainframe. If you now exit from this room and go around to the other previously locked door there is a long corridor with five guards in it, plus a piece of body armour in the locker room to the right. Both rooms will lead to the final large area with Trevelyan.

The traitor is over to the left of the room, just about to enter a lift. Sadly, even if you manage to sneak a remote mine into the lift with him, Trevelyan still makes it, so this is just a ploy to lose you some energy. Instead, just exit the level using the lift on the right wall of the final room. Congratulations.

Mission 7.3: Cuba
Level Guide Mission 7.3

Bond begins in the lift he took down from the control level. Immediately upon opening the doors, shoot the two guards in front of you and then a third and fourth who appear from

g the right. The last one has a blue hat, and this indicates that he takes more hits than anyone else. Keep pumping until he drops his gun. Turn right and you'll see the first of the many airlock-style doors, which is opening, rapidly. Blast the black guard inside before the doors have fully opened, and then run through and shoot the four or five guards who come running up the set of stairs to the right. Each one has a different gun, and here you can get the ultra-useful AR33.

At the bottom of the stairs is a walkway suspended just above the surface of the underground lake. Head around to the right and before you face them directly, blast the two sentries guarding the airlock ahead. By shooting diagonally across the walkway you avoid any enemy shooting back, since they treat all walkways as solid walls. The airlock will now probably open itself, as there is usually a guard attracted by the gunfire on the way. Don't wait for it to fully open, blast him and any others on the raised platform.

Go down the steps to the left; searching for more guards, and go over to the hole cut in the rock to the right of the bottom of the steps. This leads through to another area with scientists, but there is a guard with an AR33 with his back to you who needs putting down. Go back into the first cave and force the scientist to leave his post by waving your gun around and shooting the ground near his feet if necessary. Now destroy both the Inlet pump controls here. Enter the next cave (where you shot the guard) and do the same with the Inlet controls here. Objective one will be completed. If playing on Agent level, you do not need to do this, so just follow the guide for the directions and shortcuts. All Agents have to do is not kill scientists and escape alive.

When you're finished here, climb the steps and exit through the next airlock door. You will now be in a huge open cavern with a spiral path going up. Follow this and shoot both guards who patrol along it. At the top, switch to your AR33 and use the zoom facility to shoot the sentry guarding

Nintendo 64 A-Z of Cheats Volume 2

the door. The next room has six heavy armed guards inside, so you need to take one at a time. This is not possible if you enter the chamber, because it is so large, and they can all fire at once. Instead, open both airlock doors, stand back and to the left with your AR33 zoomed in and pick them off one by one as they appear at the doorway. To help you, there is a guard standing right in front of the door a few feet away, and he can be the first one you shoot; enticing the others to follow. You should also get an extra ZMG from one of these guys, giving you two at once.

Grab all that ammo and head around to the airlock door on the far side; ignoring all the crates. As you open this one, immediately use the zoom on the AR33 to shoot the guy right in front of you, then the one on the far left, and then prepare for three or four more who come in from the right. Shoot their heads to save bullets. Walk through and mop up any survivors, particularly the one down the gangway to the right, and perhaps another on the bottom level. Get the dropped ammo and proceed down the steps to the lower level, but instead of following the path, turn around and go round the back and left where there is a small room.

Bring up the first of your timed mines and throw it so that it lands on the row of lockers in this room. Now switch to guns. When the lockers explode, walk behind them to find a secret passage which winds to the left and right before culminating at the back of some more lockers. Mine these as well (get well back as the explosion will travel further through the tight passage. Now switch to your AR33 and peek around the corner where the lockers once were. This is the chamber where the Outlet controls are kept. Pick off the three black guards here and then run straight across the chamber to the far wall. Turn and face the stairs to your left. Zoom in with the AR33 and prepare to shoot four or five (depending on how many are alerted by the explosion) black guards as they run down to get you.

With the room cleared, shoot all the computers in this

g room (not the large pump itself though) and Objective two will be complete. Also make sure you have picked up keycard A from one of the corpses. Now cautiously walk up the stairs; keeping to the right. There is a drone gun at the top of the stairs on the right, so edge around and shoot its muzzle as soon as you can. Also be wary of the fact that sometimes there is a guard to the right who wasn't fooled into running down the stairs at you earlier. This is also true of the AR33-toting guy who can be found behind the lockers in this top section, if you haven't taken care of him already.

The blast door underneath the drone gun is locked with a keycard you don't yet have, so exit via the airlock and turn to shoot the guard waiting on the right as it opens. The double ZMG combination is best for this next section. Having felled the first guard, turn left and take out first one, then another two guards along the gangway to the left. Now go back and follow the path to the right. Around the bend you will face a very long straight with three guards on it. Use a strafing action to take care of them all. Further on you'll find a guard with his back to you at the right turn, and then another further down. Look carefully and you'll also see an airlock door over to the left, some windows, and two sentries guarding it. This is the communications area with the radio and master control console.

This is good for a laugh. Arm yourself with a timed mine, and throw it between the two sentries from the adjacent platform. Now switch to ZMGs in case one of them makes it far enough to take a shot at you. When the smoke clears, get the ammo and keycard C. Two guards may appear from the steps leading to the lower level, so watch your back and get away from the airlock to take care of them.

The best way to enter the communications area (and this has been tested time and time again) is to switch to your AR33 and backtrack along the gangway a bit so that you can see the large windows to the left of the airlock clearly. Now use the zoom to shoot them all out and hopefully rile the occupants. Now walk back along the platform to the airlock doors. Zoom in on the doors and before long the peeved guards from behind the windows will appear and run straight into your guns. One of them holds keycard B, which means you have access to Trevelyan's corridor, but more importantly, you will also get an RCP-90, which is the best automatic in the game.

Now enter the airlock with your AR33 armed and grab the only piece of body armour in the level (for Secret Agents, not OO Agents). Run to the left, turn, use the zoom, and take out the bleeder who is firing on you from across the cavern. Also be on the watch for guards emerging from the radio room and throwing grenades. Still using the AR33, peek around the corner of the radio room and pick off the four guards inside.

At this point, make sure you haven't killed any scientists, because through incompetent grenade throwing, the guards here have a tendency to blow the whole area up themselves. If playing on OO Agent level, you must get in and shoot all the guards before this happens, because then you must walk over the radio and contact Jack Wade and the CIA. If you shoot the wooden crates outside of the radio room, this sometimes lures out the guards one at a time. The master controls are in this section, so once you're done here, shoot the barrels next to the radio to torch the joint.

All that remains for you to do on this level is escape, and boy has Trevelyan got a trap for you. Basically you exit the radio area through the large blast door and shoot the two guards on station here. Now open the doors to the left and take out those two guards too, making sure you close the blast doors behind you.

Now open the airlock and stand back, as Trevelyan will start shooting. Use your AR33 to hit him, and also take out the two, count 'em two, drone guns on the ceiling in the tiny capsule beyond. When Trevelyan says "So slow, James.. yet again." It means some guards are going to try and attack you from behind, so stay sharp, and don't concentrate on the drone guns unless the coast is clear and you've closed

g   the blast doors behind you. The opening of these is a clue to when someone is sneaking up on you, hence the need for security.

The guards are never-ending here, so as soon as the drone guns are gone, and you've silenced the guards behind, open the airlock and go through, closing the doors behind you. Run through the capsule and open the far doors. Behind is a small room with three guards in it. Take these goons out with your unbeatable RCP-90 and all you have to do is enter the lift to complete the mission. No problem!

Mission 7.4: Cuba
Level Guide Mission 7.4

It's the last level, and the only thing standing between the girl, a cool drink and that final saucy wink to camera as Tina Turner kicks in, is Trevelyan. The Antenna cradle has been left high and dry by your antics with the water pumps and now you must climb all over it and battle with the MI6 traitor. Be warned though, his personal guards are swarming all over the place and they're never-ending.

You start the level on one of the far radio masts next to a tower and the first Herculanian task is to reach the Antenna itself – no mean feat when there are machine gun-toting guards standing on the thin walkway ahead. First of all walk around the tower and pick up the piece of body armour waiting for you. To get past the many guards on the walkway, you must lure them down to you. Walk a few paces down the gantry and shoot into the distance with your PP7. Retreat back to the tower and stand to the right of the gantry facing forward. When the first guard appears, wait until he is nearly on you, and then shoot him in the head. Run forward and get the fallen guard's ZMG and retreat back to the same place, as three more guards are now on the way and they have a nasty habit of being able to hit you even at this distance. Trevelyan will now set the timer to position the Antenna. You have about three minutes.

Use your ZMG to gun down the three guards, then wait

for a final one to appear before running out and getting all that ammo. Now quickly run up the gantry to the top; being careful to keep your gun aimed high just in case a rogue guard makes it to the top before you do. The key thing to remember on this level is that the enemy guards will not fire on you if you are not standing in line with them. The Antenna is made up of many walkways, but there is always an angled path which means you can fire on the guards diagonally. Take out any on the top of the Antenna, then turn left and take the first right path down into the centre of the cradle.

At the centre there is a raised platform and some steps leading below. Take out any guards in your way and run down to the steps; turning left at the bottom and heading over to the door to the hut in the top corner. There are two drone guns in this room, but the key to taking out the first one (facing the door), is to open the door and then immediately pull back out of its firing range. You can now take it out with impunity, but watch out for black guards attacking you from behind.

With the coast clear, head into the hut and shoot the drone gun to the left, before walking around the the machinery and shooting the computer console to stop the timer and the klaxon. More often than not guards will come into the hut from either side, so use the machinery as cover and employ your strafe move to shoot them. A good tip is that if you hit them just once, it delays their firing for a few seconds. Try spraying the whole group to give you some time to finish them off.

Leave the hut from the door on your left and although it looks obvious, don't go down the slope or you'll get peppered by Trevelyan. Instead, run over to the railings straight ahead, look down, and shoot Trevelyan in the head before he runs off. The more heads shots you get on this level, the quicker he will give up the chase and run down for the final showdown at the bottom of the cradle. Just winging him is not good enough here, OO7.

g With Trevelyan on the run, get down that slope before more guards arrive and head around the gangways to the other end of the platform. There is another slope here, so go up it and you'll be facing the back door to the other hut. As soon as you open the door, Trevelyan will fire on you, so do it from a hidden position and then use the strafe buttons to get some hits in. After this, Trevelyan will scarper, but he may also drop a grenade!

Trevelyan now runs up the steps, onto the raised platform in the middle of the cradle, and then up to one of the top walkways where he will stand and try to shoot you on your way up to meet him. But before you leave the hut, walk around the machinery and pick up the body armour here – you will need it!

Shoot any black guards on the way up to the top of the Antenna. When you reach the raised platform in the middle, don't head up the walkway with Trevelyan at the top. Instead go up an adjacent one and then run along to the nearest diagonal point and take your time aiming up a head shot. Treveylan will now run back down through the first hut where the drone guns were, and you must follow him all the way and follow the same pattern over and over again until he issues the final challenge "finish the job, James."

When the challenge is issued, make your way down to the bottom level of the Antenna and you'll notice in the middle that there is a set of steps leading to a small hut hanging in space. Enter this and you'll just see Trevelyan drop down the hole with the words "I was always better, James."

By now your hands will be sweating and you'll be shaking from the adrenaline, but you must arm yourself with (hopefully) twin ZMGs, point your sights slightly downward, turn so that your back is facing the hole, and then walk backwards so that you fall down it. Stop pressing the direction button immediately you start to drop, as the platform you are falling to is tiny and you can easily fall off. When you touch down, turn quickly to face Trevelyan (this has always been to the right when we've played it) and let

him have it! Don't stop shooting until the traitor is dead.
Congratulations you have won the game!

Mission 8: Teotihacan
Level Guide Mission 8.1

Initally this level is horrible. You start in a tiny alcove in front of of an Aztec decorated chamber, with three AR33-toting Drax guards. Naturally, these guys don't exactly welcome the entrance of the world's most deadly secret agent, and set about hacking divots out of you with their large calibre weapons. As soon as the level begins, turn 90° to the right (in the alcove) and press the left yellow button and forward on the stick to side-step out of your hiding place over to the right, move to the left of the giant pillar and then around to immediately shoot the gold trooper stand there. Make sure you only do this on the right side of the chamber, because the left side has two guards, and you'll be quickly over-whelmed.

Getting a good start to this level is essential, because you will need all your strength later on and there is only one piece of body armour in the whole place. Yikes! With the first guard dead, grab his AR33 and hide behind the furthest pillar from the other two. You will need to use the sniper zoom on the rifle to tag both guards, but watch out, because one has some grenades. Listen for that tell-tale 'clink' noise as they hit the floor near you – and then get the hell outta there! If you're clever, you can hide in such a way, that the grenade thrower cannot get a clear shot and bounces the grenade back on himself.

The exit is right in front of the alcove you began the level in, and is a secret door which is lighter than the rest of the surrounding wall. When opening it, watch out for a guard on the far wall in the next room, as he has his sniper zoom on, and will get a couple of good hits in before you know what's happened. Use your sneak-peek move and zoom in to shoot this guard who uses some steel crates for cover.

When firing down the corridor, make sure you're prepared

g for the two sentries on the left and right who suddenly appear and start shooting. If you are already in your zoom mode, it is a simple matter of adjusting your aim to the new threat. The next room has a large pit in the middle with a bridge across it and two more guards behind steel crates. Hide behind the convenient pillars and shoot them as soon as you can see something to shoot. These guys are also known to carry grenades.

At this point you can go down the pit to face Jaws, or, in our opinion, go through the control room which offers a far simpler way to complete the level. Once you enter the pit, you cannot get back up into this room, so make up your mind.

Still with us? Good. Open the triangular door at the end of the room and glance inside. This is the launch control room and you will see lots of monitors and black glass. The sides of the room are partitioned off and most of these areas has a gold guard in it; waiting to shoot you from the side. The way to get past this room is to shoot to one side with your AR33 and lure the ones nearby out to the door. If you stand back and to the side, using the zoom, you should be able to pick off each guard until there are no more left inside. Once you've done this, head into the room and mop up any stubborn survivors.

At the very end of the room is the shuttle guidance computer, but it is sealed behind impenetrable glass. You need the security key to open it, and this is guarded by Jaws. To your left if facing the locked room, is a computer console against the wall. Press B near this and the banks of computers to the right will drop, revealing a secret passage. Shoot the guard standing here and collect his ammo. The corridor takes a turn to the right and there are three more guards standing still to the left. Pick off each one with your AR33 and then kill two more who are standing just inside the room beyond. This is in fact the exhaust bay right beneath the boosters of the space shuttle, and if you take a step inside, a firing test will begin and eventually fry you!

Nintendo 64 A-Z of Cheats Volume 2

If you don't fancy this fate, before you enter the room, shoot out both computers on the far wall. You will notice that there are vents behind these, and once the hardware is destroyed, you can escape down either one and not get frazzled as the bay doors open above. Take note though. In order to get back to the guidance computer, you must close the bay doors first.

Before you take the right vent from the exhaust room, shoot the two guards who come down the left shaft, because one has a Moonraker laser, and this is a very powerful weapon. Now head down the right vent and follow it around. You come to a T-junction, but be warned. There are two drone guns to your left. Quickly run down the right turning and you'll find the level's only piece of body armour here.

Switch to the Moonraker laser, aim it high, and then strafe out of the shaft to shoot the two drone guns. If you miss, get back under cover quickly or they'll make mincemeat out of you! Now go up the shaft and follow it until you come a grill. This is the launch bay and it is guarded by four drone guns and a brace of guards with lasers. If you edge right up to the grating and face right, you should be able to see three of the guns, and these can be dispatched with your laser or AR33. If you need to see where they are, stick your head out and watch those bullets fly!

With three out of commission, leap out of the vent and hide behind the steel crate directly in front. Now pop out when you can and shoot the guards on the far wall – don't worry, there aren't any behind you for once. When the place is cleared, stand out of the remaining drone gun's range and finish it off. There may be a guard remaining around the corner to the right, so don't get singed by forgetting him.

Now would be a good time to climb the ladder to the left of the shaft, shoot the guard and close the bay doors so that you can head back to the guidance computers at will. With this done, exit the bay using the grating on the

g opposite wall. Ahead of you will be a series of steps leading off to the bottom left. There is a guard with his back to you here, so make sure you give him the good news in the back of the head and then head down and to the right. This will lead you to the back of the area where Jaws is waiting to give you a good hiding, But because you've taken the secret passage, both he, and all the Moonraker guards in this section, have their backs to you. Time for a sneak attack.

Fortunately, the first guard, who stands to the right of Jaws at the front of the chamber, is a bit stupid. Show your face to him for a few seconds, and for no apparent reason, he will throw a grenade which will bounce off the wall and land at his feet. If you now beat a hasty retreat, the whole area will be awash with flame in seconds, and both he and any surrounding guards will be torched. Jaws is of course unaffected.

The way to defeat Jaws without losing too much sweat is simple. Switch to the laser, stand behind him and shoot him a few times in the head. Sadly this doesn't kill him outright – it just makes him mad! Now you must run back up the first set of steps and go into the room just before the launch bay. This consists of two sets of stairs forming an 'O' shape. Get to the top of these and wait for Jaws with your laser pointing downwards. If he doesn't come, you may need to poke your head around the corner and send a few shots in his direction. When Jaws enters the 'O' room, start shooting, at his head preferably. Like the guards on the Antenna level, Jaws will only unleash the power of his two (two!) AR33s when you are in a direct line with him, so the trick is to keep running around the stairs on the opposite side to him. If you keep your laser trained on him at all times (using the strafe buttons), then Jaws will drop in no time, particularly if you notice that when he is hit, he stands still for a second or two, and this is your cue to hit him again, and again, and again (you get the picture).

Jaws is not that fast moving, and so staying at the

Nintendo 64 A-Z of Cheats Volume 2

opposite end of the stairs is a simple enough task. With Jaws gone, pick up his extra AR33 (you can now have two as well!) and the all-important keycard. Tool yourself up and then head back through the launch bay, the vents (there will be a gold trooper waiting for you where the drone guns used to be), the exhaust bay and then into the guidance control area. Note, to open the secret door, you must use the computer console to the right, or it will say it is inoperative.

Use Jaws's keycard on the glass door and it will swing open. Watch out for gold guards here, as a never-ending supply begins to come through the far door and occasionally the secret passage as well.

Activate the guidance data patch Q gave you near the computer on the left and Objective one will be completed. Also remember to take the DAT tape on the right desk, or you won't be able to launch the shuttle. With everything in place for a successful shuttle launch, blast any gold troops in your way and head back through the secret passage to the launch bay for the final stage of the mission.

Run over to the large armoured mainframe (remember those – how could you forget?) in the right corner of the launch bay and activate the DAT tape to install the launch protocol. This will start the countdown to launch, but there remains one thing you must do. Watch the vents to the left and right for approaching troops, and then leg it up the ladder to the exhaust bay door control. Activate this to open the doors and watch the glorious shuttle launch and end mission sequence. Remember though, that the countdown will stop at ten seconds if the exhaust bays doors are not open.

Mission 9: el-saghira
Level Guide Mission 9.1

A complex step-by-step guide to this level is pointless, since most of it is spent running madly after Baron Samedi, and blowing away endless regenerating goons. Basically the idea is to first fight your way past the pool of water in the opening temple and then head over to Scaramanga's trap room at the top.

The way to get through this room (one false step and the drone guns will open fire) is to follow these directions: walk left for three squares, up for two, right for four, up for three, left for one, up for one, left for one, up for three squares and then right for one. You should now be in front of the gun case and it will open as you approach (watch out for guards who unwittingly follow you into the room and set off the trap just when you're about to get the Golden Gun in the middle).

Having successfully got the Golden Gun, the hunt for Samedi can begin in earnest. This is Objective two, and as you can see, Samedi runs to three different places in rotation, a bit like Trevelyan in the Antenna level. You must keep after him, and shoot him three times in the head with the Golden Gun. You can do it with conventional weapons, but it's boring and takes ages. It's much better for Bond to finish in style. The guards in the level are just there to slow you down and sap energy, so ignore them and run away if you can. Also note that there are three pieces of body armour on this level, as Samedi is one mean boss, who can take as much as half a life bar with a single well-aimed shot. The final confrontation takes place near the last black obelisk in the corner of the level.

HEXEN (US)
Cheat Codes

Pause the game at any time, then enter the following code: C Up, C Down, C Left, C Right.

This will cause an extra menu option, 'cheat', to appear. At first none of the options can be selected – you can rectify this by entering the following additional codes.

Nintendo 64 A-Z of Cheats Volume 2

God Mode
C Left, C Right, C Down
Grants you invincibility. You'll still die from long falls, however.

Clipping
C Up (x20), C Down
Lets you walk through walls.

Visit
C Left, C Left, C Right, C Right, C Down, C Up
Level select.

Butcher
C Down, C Up, C Left, C Left
Massacres all the monsters on screen.

Health
C Left, C Up, C Down, C Down
Restores your energy to 100.

Collect All Keys
C Down, C Up, C Left, C Right

Collect All Artifacts
C Up, C Right, C Down, C Up

Collect All Weapons
C Right, C Up, C Down, C Down

Collect Puzzle Items
C Up, C Left (x3), C Right, C Down, C Down

ISS 64
Hidden Teams
On the title screen press Up, L, Up, L, Down, L, Down, L, Left, R, Right, R, Left, R, Right, R, B, A then hold Z and press Start. The phrase "What an incredible comeback!" will confirm correct code entry and six all-star teams will now be available from the team selection screen.

Big Head Players
On the title screen press C Up, C Up, C Down, C Down, C Left, C Right, C Left, C Right, B, A then hold Z and press Start. The players will now all have huge heads.

J LEAGUE PERFECT STRIKER

Hidden Teams
To get the two extra teams hidden for only the best players, go to the title screen and press the following:
Up, L, Up, L, Down, L, Down, L, Left, R, Right, R, Left, R, Right, R, B, A.
Now press Start and hold down Z.

Huge head players
On the title screen press: Yellow top, Yellow top, Yellow down, Yellow down, Yellow left, Yellow right, Yellow left, Yellow right, B, A and then press Start and hold down Z.

JOHN MADDEN 64

View Ending
Switch on the N64 and hold L, R and Z when the EA logo appears to watch the congratulatory end sequence.

Team Tiburon
In Season mode, go to the front office, select the 'create player' option and enter his name as 'Tiburon'. You can now select this team of giants in Exhibition mode!

EA Stadium
If you want to play at a hidden stadium, enter SAN MATEO on the Create Player screen. You'll now be able to play at Electronic Arts' own special ground!

Extra Teams
Again on the Create Player screen, enter the following names to access hidden teams.
SIXTIES – Players from the 1960s.
SEVENTIES – Players from the 1970s.
EIGHTIES – You'll never guess.

All Time Madden Team
Enter the name AT_MADDEN (the underscore denotes a space).

KILLER INSTINCT GOLD
Open all options

Press Z, B, A, L, A, Z on the character profiles screen. If you've done it correctly, you'll hear someone say "Perfect."

All Character Colours
To get all training colours at once, wait for the profiles to come up and press:
Z, B, A, Z, A, L.
You'll hear "Welcome" if you've done it right.

Play As Gargos
Wait until the character profiles appear and press: Z, A, R, Z, A, B. Gargos will laugh if it's worked.

Final credits
When the character profiles appear, press:
Z, L, A, Z, A, R.

Play On Sky Level
Go to the character select screen in two player mode – you must have two joypads connected. Push down on the analogue stick and press Yellow Down simultaneously on both joypads. This will let you play on a level high above the clouds.

Quack Mode
CLLTHTNMTN
A parody of Quake with bad animation and grotty textures.

Show Enemies
NSTHMNDNT
When you call up the map, enemies are shown by arrows.

Vivid Colours
LLTHCLRSFTHRNB
Changes the colour palette and makes it far more outta-sight!

Nintendo 64 A-Z of Cheats Volume 2

Gives you everything in the game!
NTHGTHDGDCRTDTRK
Weapons, invincibility, level warps, infinite ammo, big heads, the lot!

View Ending
Enter the above code, turn on the invincibility option (always handy) and warp to the Campaigner. Sort him out and the ending is yours for the watching, for as long as it lasts (not long).

KOBE BRYANT IN NBA COURTSIDE
Play Hidden Teams
From the main menu, hold L and select a pre-season game by pressing A. If you now scroll right you'll find three new teams are available.

LYLAT WARS
Medal Secrets
Each of Lylat Wars' main levels has a medal to reward the best players. To win a medal, you must achieve a certain number of hits (see Mission Guides) and also make sure all your wingmen survive to the end of the level. When you finish the game, having earnt all the medals, you'll be able to select Expert Mode. There'll also be a new sound check move to select. And if you try Versus Mode you'll find there's a new option to choose the Landmaster tank instead of an Arwing. Although slower than an Arwing, the Landmaster is 'stealthy' and won't show up on your enemies' radar screens. You must select Corneria or Katina as the battleground however, if you choose space then the

Landmaster option won't appear.

Expert Mode

Once you've earnt this option by collecting all the medals, you'll find the real challenge has only just begun.

If you select Expert Mode, you'll find Fox is wearing dark glasses, just like his father – James McCloud.

Beyond Expert

If you win a Medal on Venom 2 while playing In Expert Mode you'll be rewarded with a new end screen (Great!) and a cool new option in Versus Mode. You can now choose to control the Lylat Wars characters. Right Shift makes them run, Left Shift produces a jump while other buttons work as normal, although there doesn't seem to be a Homing Bolt. (As with the Landmaster Tank, this option won't appear if you pick a space battleground.)

If you get every Medal on Expert Mode, you get a cool new title screen!

Cheat

Although there are no cheat codes as such, the ability to replay any level (allowing another attempt to win a Medal or reach a Special Exit) offers an obvious opportunity. The game awards an extra life for every 100 points scored, so to build up extra lives simply keep replaying one of those levels where you're confident of getting 200 points or more. Similarly, if you're doing badly chasing after a Medal or exit, it's always best to play through to the end so your points score can be totalled and extra lives added before choosing the restart level option.

MACE: THE DARK AGE

Change Character Costumes
Highlight the character you want to use and press L or R, C Up, C Down, C Left, and C Right for five different costume colour schemes.

Two Player Practice Mode
Highlight Practice on the menu screen and press Start simultaneously on both controllers. Select the desired characters, and knock each other about for as long as you like with no death! (Boring!)

Fight As Grendal
Win three times in two player mode, then on the select screen for the fourth match, highlight the Executioner, hold Start and Grendal appears. Don't release start, and press Quick to select Grendal.

Fight As Gar Gunderson, The War Mech Or Ichiro
When the first screen appears when you turn the power on, rotate the analogue joystick in an anticlockwise direction from the right and you'll hear a chime. Gar Gunderson and Ichiro will appear on the character selection screen above the Executioner.

Fight As Pojo The Chicken
Successfully perform Taria's execution (doing it in two player mode is easiest). Then begin another match and highlight Taria, hold the Start button down on the selection screen and Pojo will appear. Without releasing Start, press a Quick button to select Pojo. If you're in two player select mode,

they can do the same thing and it'll be Pojo against Pojo!

Select Start Stage
Highlight the desired fighter on the character selection screen and press the Start button four times to compete on their home stage, then select the character you want to fight and begin.

Bonus Stages
To play on the bonus stages, highlight each of the characters listed in order and press Start every time, then select the character you want to play with. The following codes are for two player mode, except for Random AI

Stage	Characters
Mini Golf Course	Koyasha, Mordus Kull, Takeshi
Grendal's stage	Namira, Koyasha, Taria
Grendal's stage	Mordus Kull, Taria, Ragnar
Big heads	Koyasha, Al' Rashid, Takeshi
Small characters Long	Takeshi, Al' Rashid, Ragnar, Xiao
Random AI Namira	Hell Knight, Xiao Long, Dregan,
Speed Grid	Ichiro, Xiao Long, Koyasha
San Francisco Rush	Xiao Long, Al Rashid, Koyasha
Macchu Picchu	Namira, Koyasha, Taria

The following cheats are entered in two player mode:

Fight As Ned The Janitor
On the character selection screen, press Start on each of the following characters in turn; Koyasha, Excecutioner, Lord Deimos, then move to Xiao Long and press Quick to play as a janitor!

Head Swap
On the character selection screen, press Start on each of the following characters in turn; Al-Rashid, Takeshi, Mordos Kull, Xiao Long, Namira. The two characters that are then chosen with swap heads.

Pink Slippers
On the character selection screen, press Start on each of the following characters in turn; Ragnar, Dregan, Koyasha. When you choose a fighter, he or she will engage in combat wearing fuzzy rabbit slippers!

MAJOR LEAGUE BASEBALL (KEN GRIFFEY JR)

Bonus Teams
Highlight 'Exhibition' and repeatedly tap all the C buttons together until you hear a noise to confirm that the code has been entered correctly. You'll now be able to access the Nintendo and Angel Studios teams from the 'All-Star teams' option.

Fireworks
Access 'View Stadium' mode by pressing Z on the stadium selection screen, then press R & Z to launch some fireworks.

Control Title Screen Baseball
Hold Z on the title screen to stop the baseball spinning, then, still holding Z, move the analogue stick to control it.

MIKE PIAZZA'S STRIKE ZONE

Cheat Menu
On the pre-game menu enter L, R, L, R. You'll need to activate this code before any of the others will work.

Bonus Stadium
On the pre-game menu enter Right, A, C Up, L, A.

Always Hit Home Runs
On the pre-game menu enter L, A, Down, Right.

Crazy Ball
On the pre-game menu enter C Right, A, Z, B, A, L, L.

Crazy Pitches
On the pre-game menu enter C Right, A, Z, C Up, R, B.

Varied Pitches
On the pre-game menu enter C Right, A, Z, C Up, R, L.

Easy Steals
On the pre-game menu enter C Left, A, Down, C Up, Z.

Aluminum Bats
On the pre-game menu enter R, A, Z, B, A, L, L.

Red Bats
On the pre-game menu enter R, Down, B, A, Right.

Blue Bats
On the pre-game menu enter B, L, B, A, Right.

Nintendo 64 A-Z of Cheats Volume 2

Psychedelic Bats
On the pre-game menu enter Z, B, R, A.

Low Gravity
On the pre-game menu enter Up, R, A, L.

Increased Gravity
On the pre-game menu enter Up, Down, L, Up, R.

Fast Game
On the pre-game menu enter L, A, Z, R, B, A, L, L.

Slow Game
On the pre-game menu enter Up, L, L, B, A, L, L.

Alternate Sky
On the pre-game menu enter C Right, A, Z, C Up, L, R, Z.

Bonus Teams
On the pre-game menu enter C Right, A, Down, Left.

Hidden Message
On the pre-game menu enter C Up, R, B, B.

View Credits
On the pre-game menu enter R, A, Z, R, C Right, A, B.

MISSION IMPOSSIBLE
Complete Mission Guide
Mission 1
Objectives
1: Change identity
2: Find excuse for errand
3: Get to subpen with Clutter

m Jump up the pile of crates by the fence and drop into the base. Head left to the first hut and go inside. If you've done this quickly, there will be an old bloke inside – if not, wait for him to return (he's probably gone for a pee). After giving him a feeble explanation of your presence, blow him away and use the facemaker. Pick up the excuse from the desk.

Disguised as the soldier, go left as you leave the hut and head through the main gate, then go right. Give the excuse to the soldier hanging around the truck, then go down the alley to meet Clutter. Run to the back of the truck and jump in.

Mission 2
Objectives
1: Find magnetic mines
2: Give mine to Clutter
3: Join Dowey for getaway

Head for the red dot on the scanner to reach the pumphouse – inside, on a shelf at the back of the room, are the mines. Go out and find Clutter by following the green dot on the radar. Once he's moaned about your poor choice of mines, head back to the dock and go down the steps and use the mine when you're standing next to the gunboat. Then head for the green dot to jump aboard your escape craft as the place goes 'poof' behind you.

Mission 3
Objectives
1: Find facemaker
2: Find score
3: Find nausea powder
4: Find drink
5: Place smoke generators
6: Assume Ambassador's Aide's ID
7: Access restricted area

Talk to the couple in front of you until the man walks off – the woman is Sarah, your contact. Keep talking to her until

Nintendo 64 A-Z of Cheats Volume 2

she offers you the facemaker. Make sure there are no guards in the hall (if you're seen taking the facemaker, you'll be arrested) and get the gadget.

To find the score, first talk to the couple examining the portrait, then head for the ballroom and talk to the piano player. He'll whinge that somebody's nicked the score for the aide's favourite tune. Go back to the couple, who are now sitting down, and talk to the man. He'll stand up and waffle on about you looking like a certain short-arsed, big-nosed film star. Ignore him and walk to his chair to pick up the score.

Go back to the ballroom and talk to the barman – he is Dieter, one of your agents. He'll give you a drink (which Ethan rather stupidly puts in his pocket!) and the nausea powder. You might have noticed a woman in red standing around. This is Scofield, the enemy agent who's been sent to kill you. To get rid of her, head for the toilets, select the blowpipe, and pop a dart in her eye before she shoots you. Once you've dragged her into the cubicle, close the door to make sure nobody spots her.

Now, head back to the ballroom and give the score to the piano player. The aide will come strutting down the stairs to listen to his beloved national anthem. Give him the poisoned drink, then follow him to the toilets as he rushes off to yak. Chin him, hide him in the other cubicle, then use the facemaker.

Next, you have to plant the smoke generators to prepare for your escape. The vents you need to plant them in are shown on the radar as white dots. Make sure that there aren't any guards watching when you drop them – again, if you're seen, you'll be arrested.

All but one of the vents are on the ground floor. The last one is at the top of the stairs, to the left. Plonk it in there, then run to the other end of the hall and enter the lift.

Mission 4
Objectives
1: Find exit key

2: Access KGB HQ

Exit the lift, deck the guard and steal his gun. You need the weapon to shoot out the many crates that block your path. Unfortunately, shooting the crates also releases toxic gas!

Temporary respite can be had by finding the first-aid boxes on the walls and eating the pills inside, but for protection you need a 'geek suit'. This is hidden in the crate marked with a biohazard symbol to the right after the first pair of large crates. Just walk into it and put it on.

Taking care to pick off the numerous guards infesting the cellars (make sure you collect their ammo – you'll need it), make your way around the level. Although you don't need to destroy the crates with the satellite parts on Possible level, they're a useful marker, as one of the guards near the crates will drop the vital exit key when killed. The particular guard is chosen randomly, so you need to search until you find it. When you've got the key, go to the exit – it's the white dot on the scanner.

Mission 5
Objectives

1: Talk to Barnes
2: Find video freezer
3: Find facemaker
4: Find dartgun
5: Sabotage video link
6: Find exit passcard
7: Get transfer order
8: Escape with Candice

Go left as you leave the lift, passing the double doors with the guard outside, and enter the room at the far end of the hall where you'll find Barnes croaking his last and building up his part. Leave the room, go left again and go to the room on your left at the end of the hall. Inside this storeroom, on one of the shelves, is the facemaker.

Leave the room, go back to the guarded door and talk to the guard – he will now let you in. Inside is the KGB security chief. Punch him out, hide his body behind the desk and use the facemaker.

Collect the dartgun from his desk, then leave the room. The guards waiting outside will believe his story that he's arrested the intruder and return to their normal duties. Go down the corridor ahead and enter the door on the right. Inside is Candice's cell and a guard. Pick up the video freezer from the desk, then return to the chief's office.

Go to the model train on the left wall. Push the button and the picture will slide back to reveal another button. Push it, then turn around and enter the secret room. Go in, take out both the guards, and pick up the exit passcard. Use the video freezer on the equipment in the corner, then exit the room, turn left as you leave the chief's office and continue round to the room with the white door.

Inside, talk to the man, who will give you the transfer orders. Go back to Candice's cell and give the orders to the guard. Once you've explained the situation, walk (don't run – Candice can't keep up, and will be caught if she's unaccompanied) to the metal doors near the lift. Use the passcard on the card reader to escape.

Mission 6
Objectives
1: Secure passage for Candice
2: Activate master switch

A very annoying level, but it's got to be done. The floor tiles are electrically charged – the dangerous ones glow red for a short time. Since some of the five sets of electric floor change with each game, they can't be mapped – you'll need to be quick to get across before the glow fades.

Make sure that you kill all the guards as you go – if any are left alive, Candice will be captured. When you reach the end of the level, hit the master switch to turn off the floors. Candice will then join you.

Mission 7
Objectives
1: Find super-computer
2: Protect Candice
3: Get NOC list
4: Escape

Go through the metal door when Candice opens it, shoot the guard and go left into the sewage plant. Hop onto the moving platform, ride it across and kill the guard in front of you. Hit the switch he was guarding to lower a section of catwalk, then jump back on the moving platform and go down the newly-opened walkway. Turn left and go through the steel door, shoot the guard and hit the button. This will open up another walkway – leave the room and go all the way down the corridor ahead until you enter a small room.

Hit the button on the console to open the computer room door – this also starts a countdown, so you need to be quick. Head back to the sewage plant, making sure you let Candice catch up with you every so often. Go back across the moving platform, zapping any guards who pop up, and go left as you leave the plant. The computer room door has opened on your left in the short brick passage. Go in, kill the guards, and run up to the computer. Wait for Candice to arrive (she may have problems with a guard outside – if so, nip out and waste him) and get the NOC list, then head back to the room where you started the level to escape.

Mission 8
Objectives 1
1: Secure passage for Candice
2: Find the mask of Golytsine

Objectives 2
1: Unfreeze video cameras
2: Assume Golytsine's identity
3: Find exit key
4: Escape with Candice

Nintendo 64 A-Z of Cheats Volume 2

The Goldeneye left-over drone guns in the ceiling are now active – use the pistol to snipe them out from the end of each corridor. When you reach the control panel at the far end, wait for Candice to arrive – if you activate it too soon, she'll be fried by the electric floors.

Enter the room that opens up next to you. As the doors close, Candice will be captured, but you can worry about her later. Open the cabinet to get the mask, then smash the control panel next to it. The doors at each end of the room will open and guards pour in. Shoot them all, then leave though the door you entered by. Go back up the corridor, and a guard will leg it from a room on the left. Ignore him for now – go into the room and help Candice. Head back along the security corridor and kill anything in a peaked cap. One of them will drop the NOC list – pick it up, then go back to the double doors at the opposite end of the complex.

When Candice arrives, you'll find yourself back in KGB headquarters. Put on the mask, then race to the secret room and grab the video freezer. The next time you're caught on camera, this will implicate Golytsine. Leg it to the room with the white door, put one between the guard's eyes and swipe the exit key. Then just head for the smoking double doors and use the key to leave.

Mission 9
Objectives 1
1: Secure access to the lift
2: Find Jack
3: Dress as fireman
4: Give Candice fireman outfit
5: Escape the embassy

The embassy is in chaos as your smoke bombs fill the place with fumes. Shoot the two guards on the upper corridor, and Candice will hide in the lift. Go down the stairs and talk to one of the firemen – it's Jack in disguise. He'll race off to the toilets.

Try to avoid having any of the guards see you with Jack

on the way to the lavvies – if they realise you're in cahoots, the jig is up! If you want to conserve ammo, you can use the fire extinguishers to kill the guards.

In the bogs, talk to Jack to get the fireman's outfit, then (in your cunning disguise) go back to the lift and give the spare outfit to Candice. Assuming you haven't been discovered – you'll know if you have, as a message will warn you – you can just saunter out of the exit without a care.

Mission 10
Objectives 1
1: Escape from interrogation
2: Pick up the equipment
3: Get into hallway

Objectives 2
1: Get out of interrogation sector
2: Take free access print
3: Find sergeant for exit access
4: reach elevator to infirmary

Objectives 3
1: Find the antidote
2: Distract attention
3: Find way to roof

The CIA obviously don't have much confidence in their agents – for successfully completing his assignment, Ethan is arrested on suspicion of being a traitor!

You start the level locked in a cell. On the wall with the door is a hard-to-see switch – push it to open the shutter hiding the window. When the intercom sounds, activate it to talk to Candice, then get the gum from under the mug and use it on the window. Stand well back!

Climb out of the shattered window and collect all your kit, then head for the door. Outside, you have to sit through some exposition – when it's over, a countdown starts. You

Nintendo 64 A-Z of Cheats Volume 2

have ten minutes to escape the building.

Shoot the marine at the desk, then use the fingerprint scanner on him and press the button on the wall. The doors will open. Run through and race to the end of the corridor. Behind the crates to your left is a can of spray paint, which you can use to blind the security cameras. It goes without saying that you should also be nailing any guards you encounter!

Continue around the corridor until you find the last pair of marines at a door. Use the fingerprint scanner on their twitching bodies, then go back to the rotating door (the large diagonal barrier at one corner) and push the button twice to nip through into a small office area. Grab the empty gun from the desk and head for the next revolving door. On the other side is a geeky bloke at a desk. Drop him with the dartgun or a stunner before he can raise the alarm, zap the guard at the far end of the corridor, then switch to the empty gun and enter the small office. Threaten the fat bloke with the gun, and follow him to the double doors at the end of the corridor. When he's opened the door, stun him and go inside.

The drugged coffee now takes effect – just walking becomes a major effort. Go left into the lift, then close the doors and ride down to the infirmary level. Put away any weapons you may be holding, go in and talk to the nurse to your right. She'll helpfully give you the antidote. Once you're as right as rain, you need to create a diversion. You have a choice – you can either push the button to slam the poor bloke on the bed into the ceiling, or rev up the running machine and send the other chap flying. Either way, the nurses will be suitably distracted and you can nip out of the window.

Mission 11
Objectives
1: Sabotage heliport lights
2: Find bag of equipment
3: Find zone digitcards

4: Fix lights
5: Paralyse helicopter with EMS
6: Enter security level
7: Find security level code
8: Meet Candice

On the roof, make sure you finish talking to Candice, then go around the corner with your dartgun out. Pop the guard and take his access card, then climb up the side of the guard post and head for the control box ahead. Turn off the electric floor, then head around the balcony to the next control box. This will switch off the helipad lights.

Drop back down and continue around, using the access card to open the gates. Nip into the guard posts to collect extra ammo as you go. When you reach the fence, climb up the guard post onto the next level, where you'll find the bag of equipment.

Use the bag and you miraculously and not at all suspiciously become a repairman. Put away your weapon and make your way to the first door you find. Enter it and you'll be magically teleported to the roof. Cross the bridge and wait for the guard to let you in.

Once inside, go down the ramp to the left, kill the guard and take anything he drops, and turn the power back on. Quickly head back up and run for where the helicopter is landing. Beyond the helipad is a control box – use the EMS to jam the radar and keep the chopper grounded.

Go down the other ramp and kill the guard to get his digitcard, then go through the door. At the end of the short passage, turn left to face the wall, aim your gun, then quickly sidestep into the open and shoot the guard. If you're too slow, you'll be arrested. Get his security card and go through the gate.

Around the next corner is a stack of crates. Climb to the top, shoot the guard on the next level, then use the infra-red contact lenses to see the laser beams. Use the deflector to open a gap in the beams, then drop down and go left.

Around the corner is a security post. Climb the crates and

Nintendo 64 A-Z of Cheats Volume 2

leave the camera on top of them to watch the code panel, then go back around the corner and wait until you get the 'code obtained' message. Go back, collect the camera, and enter the building to meet Candice.

Mission 12
Objectives
1: Switch on the computer
2: Get the NOC list
3: Escape

First change the camera angle with the C buttons so you can judge the perspective, then carefully lower yourself. If you keep the stick pushed forward so you descend head-first, you minimise your chances of being singed by a laser.

When you reach the yellow laser beams, hang just above them for a moment and they'll obligingly move aside. Drop past quickly, even if this means taking damage. There are three yellow lasers in all.

At the bottom of the shaft, you'll be told when you're at the right height to reach the card reader. Turn around so you're facing the door, then swing back and forth until you can reach it. It can take quite a while to get the rhythm right – either be patient, or throw the cartridge in the bin! Once you've reached the card reader and locked the door, lower yourself slightly until you get the message that you're at the right height. Turn to face the computer, then swing again until you reach it. Now you just have to wait for the cutscene to run its course – the instant you can move, head back up to the top of the shaft before you get caught!

Mission 13
Objectives
1: Join heliport
2: Unactivate EMS
3: Escape with helicopter

It's bizarre use of the English language time with these objectives! Put in the IR lenses, then jump over the railings (taking care not to land near a guard and get arrested) until you reach the laser level. Find the crate next to the beams, climb up it and jump over the lasers. You may take damage, but you'll survive. Go right and plant some gum on the pipes to create a diversion, then either run and shoot your way back to the narrow passage, or take the long way around to avoid trouble. There is a guard right around the corner at the far end of the passag, on the other side of the door – carefully sidestep until he's visible, then shoot him before he arrests you.

Run up to the heliport ('join' it, if you will) and go to the control panel. Get the EMS, then use it again to 'unactivate' it. Run to the helicopter and climb aboard as it takes off.

Mission 14
Objectives
1: Protect Ethan
2: Take the train

Arms dealer Max has double-crossed Ethan, so, as a pair of snipers in the rafters of Waterloo station, you have to take out her many, many henchmen and women so that Ethan can reach the train.

Use B to switch between snipers when your view is blocked. The only thing you need to do is be careful not to shoot any civilians, or it's game over!

Mission 15
Objectives
1: Neutralise Max's henchmen
2: Meet Candice
3: Find switch to block exits
4: Knock out Max's bodyguards
5: Stop Max and seize NOC list
6: Defuse Max's backup plan

You have to kill all of Max's goon squad, so make sure you collect any ammo they drop and try to take them out with a single headshot to save time.

Nintendo 64 A-Z of Cheats Volume 2

When you find Candice, she'll give you a gizmo that lets you block off the rear half of the train (in other words, saves memory by chopping the level into two separate halves – cunning, huh?). Push the button, then go through the door. Don't kill the dork blocking your path – just talk to him and he'll move aside.

At the far end of the carriage, on the left, is a train attendant. Talk to him, beat the crap out of him (sorry, mate) and use the facemaker to disguise yourself. Put away your gun, and you'll be able to wander through the hit squad in the next carriage with impunity. Max is in the end compartment – lob the gas canister inside, stand back as she's knocked out, then pick up the detonator and NOC list. A countdown will start, but you don't need to worry – yet.

The next carriage houses a bar, but Jim Phelps's mind isn't on duty free – he's revealed as the traitor! Unfortunately, everyone in the bar is on his side. Kill them all and follow Phelps into the baggage car. Kill his henchmen, then pick up the blowtorch and liquid nitrogen – gee, kinda convenient that they were just lying around, huh? – and go to the safe at the far end.

To open the safe, first of all use the blowtorch on one hinge, stopping when it turns red-hot (heat it too much and the bomb – and train – will explode), then spray it with liquid nitrogen until it shatters. Repeat this on the other hinge, then open the safe and use the detonator to deactivate the bomb. After this, just go back and finish off Max's remaining thugs to complete the level.

Mission 16
Objectives
1: Catch Phelps

Taking care not to touch the electrified pantograph arms on the raised sections, make your way down the train. Shoot the first goon and pick up his handy pocket-sized rocket launcher, then use this (carefully – ammo is limited) to take out the cars and helicopters carrying Phelps's seemingly infinite army of associates. Occasionally, a helicopter will buzz the length of the train and try to knock you off – either duck or move to one side. When you reach the last carriage of the train, or it enters the Channel Tunnel, Phelps jumps onto the skids of a helicopter. When this happens, you have less than 20 seconds to bring down the chopper before he escapes.

Mission 17
Objectives
1: Get the AF Scrambler
2: Get the mine
3: Bring Clutter AFS and mine
4: Get the gas injector
5: Get the RC detonator
6: Get the explosives
7: Sabotage the pump house
8: Regroup on the comm building

Max's associates are completing an arms deal at the submarine base you infiltrated at the start of the game, and it's up to the IMF to stop it.

From your drop point, go around the dock to the right and climb up the crates to get the AFS, then go to each of the red dots on the radar in turn to collect the other four pieces of your scattered equipment. When you've got it all, go back to the dock and give it to Clutter, then head for the pump house (you visited it in the second mission). One of the useless berks on your team will complain that he's lost his wirecutters. Luckily, there's a pair in the pumphouse, at the back. Once you've got them, drop your explosives in the pump room and go around the back of the building to deliver the precious wirecutters before using the detonator to destroy the pumps.

Head for the communications building (it's got a huge golf ball on the roof, so you can't miss it) and climb up the crates at the side. Your team are involved in a shootout. Help them out, and they'll jump onto a passing truck and escape.

Nintendo 64 A-Z of Cheats Volume 2

Before you can escape yourself, you need the night vision goggles – these are in a hut full of terrorists! Once you've found them, climb back onto the roof of the comm building and jump onto the next available truck.

Mission 18
Objectives
1: Find explosives
2: Sabotage anchor bolts

Jump over the chains and duck under the ventilators and lights, and make sure you leap onto each platform before you get scraped off on the supports. The explosives are at the end of the first platform, so don't miss them.

The anchor bolts are easy to find – there's one at each side of the supports. Drop some explosives on each one, go through the door and take out any guards you may encounter, then jump onto the next truck. Repeat the sequence until all the anchor bolts have been mined, then hop aboard a truck and leave the tunnel as it explodes.

Mission 19
Objectives
1: Find explosives and plastic
2: Sabotage power plant
3: Cut off camera power
4: Take on accountant's ID
5: Get briefcase from bunker
6: Sabotage briefcase
7: Bring briefcase to deal
8: Blow away helicopter
9: Escape on gunboat with Clutter

Head for the white dot on the radar, which is a hole in the fence – go through it and jump onto the tunnel mouth to cross the river. On the other side, climb up the crates onto the roof of the building, shoot the guards and drop down. Head for the green dot and Clutter will give you the explosives. To get back across the river, look for the hole in the fence to the right of the building and climb back to the roof.

The power plant is the collection of towers and transformers – head left after crossing the river. Drop the explosives here, then go behind the small guard hut to the box on the wall – this is the circuit breaker. Stick the plastic explosive to it, then shoot it to knock out the video cameras and searchlights. As a parting shot, get clear then detonate the explosives to wipe out the power plant.

Go into the hut you passed on the way from the river (there's a video camera over the door) and kill the accountant. Pick up his ID and use the facechanger, then put away any weapons. Cross the river again, traverse the building, and this time go in through the front door. The guard will wave you through. Use the accountant's ID to open the vault, then go in and blag the briefcase.

Go back to Clutter and he will, in a microsecond, rig the briefcase with a bomb. Continue past him to the helipad and follow its occupants into the building. Make the deal, and wait until everyone has left the room. Switch to the sniper rifle and pick off the guards behind the building. The helicopter will explode just after takeoff – once it's in bits, wait for Clutter to arrive, then go to the gunboat and escape.

Mission 20
Objectives
1: Escape enemy base
2: Destroy gas factory

Use the gunboat's twin cannon to blast everything on the sides of the river, targeting bunkers and gun emplacements first, and also picking off any mines when Clutter yells a warning. Two other gunboats will try to block you – just pump a couple of dozen rounds into their cabins and they'll quickly pay a visit to Davey Jones's Locker. Near the end of the river, two high walls mark the boundary of the gas plant. Pick off the gun turrets, then keep firing at the walls and chimneys until they cave in. Once the whole complex is in ruins, the world is saved and Ethan Hunt gets to snog the heroine atop a submarine. Woohoo!

MORTAL KOMBAT 4

Alternate Costumes
Rotate the select screen pictures twice to access each character's second outfit. Sonya and Tanya's pictures must be rotated three times.

Cheat Option
Highlight 'Continue' on the options screen then hold Run and Block until the cheat option appears.

Fight As Goro
Select the invisible icon on the character selection screen. Press Up, Up, Up, highlight Shinnok's icon and press Run and Block.

Fight As Noob Saibot
Select the invisible icon on the character selection screen. Press Up, Up, highlight Reiko's icon and press Run and Block.

Kombat Kodes
Input the following codes on the two-player 'Vs' screen where the character pictures are displayed facing each other. There are two three-digit displays at the bottom of the screen. The first three correspond to the buttons on controller one, the second to the buttons on controller two. The numbers indicate how many times you must press Low Punch, Block and Low Kick respectively:
001 001 Unlimited Run
002 002 Weapon Kombat
010 010 Disable Maximum Damage
012 012 Noob Saibot

020 020 Red Rain
050 050 Explosive Kombat
100 100 Throwing Disabled
110 110 Maximum Damage and Disabled Throws
111 111 Free Weapon
123 123 No Power
222 222 Random Weapons
321 321 Big Head Mode
333 333 Random Kombat
444 444 Armed and Dangerous
555 555 Many Weapons
666 666 Silent Kombat

More Kombat Kodes

As before, you need to input the following codes on the two-player Vs screen where the character pictures are displayed facing each other. Use Low Punch, Block and Low Kick on the controllers in port one and port two to alter the numbers in the boxes. The following codes will allow you to fight on any level you choose:

Goro's Lair	011 011
The Well	022 022
Elder God's stage	033 033
Tomb Stage	044 044
Rain Stage	055 055
Snake Stage	066 066
Shaolin Temple	101 101
Living Forest	202 202
Prison	303 303
Ice Pit	313 313

Cheat Options Menu

Highlight the "continues" line on the options screen then hold C Right and C Down until the cheat menu appears.

Nintendo 64 A-Z of Cheats Volume 2

Automatic First Fatalities
Enable the cheat menu, then turn on Fatalities I. When the finish message appears, do an uppercut to perform any character's first fatality.

Automatic Second Fatalities
Enable the cheat menu and turn on Fatalities II. When the finish message appears, do an uppercut to perform any character's second fatality.

Automatic Endings
Enable the cheat menu and turn on Endings. Then simply defeat one opponent in arcade mode to see the ending for your character.

MORTAL KOMBAT MYTHOLOGIES: SUB-ZERO

View Credits
Was printed as GRVDTS – but should have been CRVDTS. The offending writer has had his heart ripped out. In an attempt to make amends (grovel, grovel) here are some more cheats for those of you too rubbish to reach the end of the game.

Skip To Quan Chi
As Sub-Zero dies before a checkpoint, hold down A.

Skip To Shinnok
As Sub-Zero dies before a checkpoint, hold down B.

Beating Shinnok
Shinnok has an impenetrable shield that works even if he's

frozen, but he can be defeated. As he fires a blast at you his shield will drop for a second, at which point you need to throw an ice blast. If you've got the timing right, he'll be frozen, but you still can't reach him. Instead, freeze him again, and run back to the teleporter, which will take you to the teleporter behind Shinnock. Quickly run up to him, as his shield only functions from the front, and press A to grab Shinnock's medallion. If you're successful, Shinnok will transform into a monster and Rayden's portal will appear. Jump through the portal to meet Rayden and Shang Tsung.

Combos
3 Hit – requires 18 experience pts:
HK, HK, Back + HK
6 Hit – requires 36 experience pts:
HP, HP, LP, LK, HK, Back + HK

Special Moves
1. Ice Blast: Down, Forward, LP
2. Slide: BL + LP + LK + Back
3. Directional Ice Blast
Upwards: Down, Forward, HK
Downwards: Down, Back, LK
4. Air Ice Blast: Jump, then Down, Forward, LP
5. Ice Clone: Down, Back, LP
6. Ice Shatter: Freeze twice, then Uppercut or Roundhouse Kick
7. Super Slide: BL, LP, HP, Back
8. Freeze On Contact: Down, Forward, Forward, HP
9. Polar Blast: Forward, Back, Back, HP
Fatality
Spine Rip: Forward, Down, Forward, HP
You need to be one step away to accomplish this move.

Passwords
Enter the following codes on the password screen for useful results:

Nintendo 64 A-Z of Cheats Volume 2

NXCVSZ – Will give you unlimited urns
GTTBHR – Grants you 1000 lives
ZCHRRY – Start with 20,000 experience points at the Fortress
CRVDTS – This code lets you view the credits

Level Codes
Wind – THWMSB
Earth – CNSZDG
Water – ZVRKDM
Fire – JYPPHD
Prison – RGTKCS
Bridge – QFTLWN
Fortress – XJKNZT

Fatality
Spine Rip: Forward, Down, Forward, HP
You need to be one step away to accomplish this move.

Invincibility
Enter TDFCLT on the password screen.

MORTAL KOMBAT TRILOGY

Random Character
On the character select screen, put the cursor over Noob Saibot and press Up and Start simultaneously for a completely random selection.

Choose Battle Arena
On the character select screen, highlight Sonya and press Up and Start. An earthquake will occur and then you will be able to select the course.

Play as Motaro
On Jade's Desert, Wasteland or Kahn's Tower, press and hold the analogue stick left and then press A and the Yellow top button before the match begins. Your fighter should explode and Motaro will replace him.

Play as Shao Kahn
On the Rooftop or Pit 3, press Down on the analogue stick and press A and B before the start of the bout. Shao Kahn will appear.

Play as Khameleon
On the Star Bridge stage, when the annoying gonk appears in the bottom corner of the screen and squeals "Toasty!", just press Down and Start before he vanishes from whence he came. You'll then have the opportunity to battle our poorly-spelt chum.

Fight asHuman Smoke
Choose Cyber-Ninja Smoke as a character. Then hold ⇐ + HP + HK + Run + Block before the 'Fight' screen appears or inbetween rounds. Cyber-Ninja Smoke will explode and change into Human Smoke.

Unlimited kredits
During the story screen, press ⇩, ⇩, ⇧, ⇧, ⇨, ⇨, ⇐, ⇐. A sound will confirm that the code has worked. Now after the next match is lost, the word 'Freeplay' will appear in the remaining Kredits window.

Extra options
During the Kombat Mode selection screen, press ⇧ + Start. Now new options to disable timer, blood, aggressor and kombos will appear.

Nintendo 64 A-Z of Cheats Volume 2

Bonus Galaga-type game
If you persevere and fight 100 two-player matches consecutively, a game called Land Of Rellim will begin.

Bonus Pong game
Not quite as gruelling, but if you fight 50 two-player matches consecutively, a bonus game of Pong will start running.

Bonus SpaceInvaders-typegame
Press Z when an object appears over the moon on the pit stage of a two-player match. The sound of a bell will confirm that the code has worked. The winner of that round will play Invaders From Space.

Enable both redand blue ? menus
During the story screen, press HK, LK, Run, LP, HP, HP, HP, LP, LP very quickly. If the code has worked, a sound will be heard. Now the red and blue question mark menus will be available to provide the following options:

Red Question Mark menu

Freeplay	ON/OFF
Fatality Time	ON/OFF
Collision Boxes	ON/OFF
One Round Matches	ON/OFF

Blue Question Mark menu

Level Select	ON/OFF
Throwing	ENABLED/DISABLED
Unlimited Run	ENABLED/DISABLED
Bloody Kombat	ON/OFF
Human Smoke	ON/OFF
Khameleon	ON/OFF

 ## COMPLETE MOVES LIST!

Baraka
Blade Spark: D, B, HP
Blade Swipe: B+HP
Shredder: B, B, B, LP
Blade Spin: F, D, F, Block repeatedly
Fatality (close): B, B, B, HP
Fatality (close): B, F, D, F, LP
Animality (close): Hold HP, F, B, D, F, release HP
Friendship: D, F, HK
Babality: F, F, F, HK
Brutality: HP, HP, HP, LP, LP, Block, HK, HK, LK, LK, Block
Stage: LK, Run, Run, Run, Run
Standard Combo: HP, HP, B+HP, D+HP

Cyrax
Close Grenade: Hold LK, B, B, HK
Far Grenade: Hold LK, F, F, HK
Net: B, B, LK
Teleport: F, D, Block Air
Throw: D, F, Block, LP
Fatality: D, D, U, D, HP
Fatality (close): D, D, F, U, Run
Animality (close): U, U, D, D
Friendship: Run, Run, Run, U
Babality: F, F, B, HP
Brutality: HP, HK, HP, HK, HK, HP, HK, HP, HK, LK, LP
Stage: Run, Block, Run
Standard Combo: HP, HP, HK, HP, HK, B+HK

Jade
Boomerang (high): B, F, HP
Boomerang: (middle): B, F, LP
Boomerang (low): B, F, LK
Boomerang (returning): B, B, F, LP

Projectile Invincibility: B, F, HK
Glow Kick: D, F, LK
Fatality (close): U, U, D, F, HP
Fatality (close): Run, Run, Run, Block, Run
Animality (close): F, D, F, F, LK
Friendship: B, D, B, B, HK
Babality: D, D, F, D, HK
Brutality: HP, LK, HP, LP, HK, HK, LK, Block, Block, HP, HK
Stage: B, F, D+Run
Standard Combo: HP

Jax
Missile: B, F, HP
2 Missiles: F, F, B, B, HP
Gotcha Grab: F, F, LP repeatedly
Backbreaker (in air): Block
Quad Slam: HP repeatedly
Ground Pound: Hold LK, then release
Dashing Punch: F, F, HK
Fatality (close): U, D, F, U, Block
Fatality (far): Run, Block, Run, Run, LK
Animality (close): Hold LP, F, F, D, F, release LP
Friendship: LK, Run, Run, LK
Babality: D, D, D, LK
Brutality: HP, HP, HP, Block, LP, HP, HP, HP, Block, LP, HP
Stage: D, F, D, LP
Standard Combo: HK, HK, D+HP, HP, Block, LP, B+HP

Johnny cage
High Fireball: F, D, B, HP
Low Fireball: B, D, F, LP
Green Shadow Kick: B, F, LK
Red Shadow Kick: B, B, F, HK
Shadow Uppercut: B, D, B, HP
Fatality (close): D, D, F, F, LP
Fatality (half screen): D, D, F, F, LK
Friendship: D, D, D, D, LK

Animality (sweep): D, F, F, HK
Babality: F, B, B, HK
Stage: D, B, F, F, HK
Brutality: HP, LK, HK, LP, HP, HK, HK, HP, HP, LP, HP
Standard Combo: HP, HP, LP, D+LP

Kabal
Top Spin: B, F, LK Eye
Spark: B, B, HP
Ground Saw: B, B, B, Run
Fatality (sweep): D, D, B, F, Block
Fatality (close): Run, Block, Block, Block, HK
Animality (close): Hold HP, F, F, D, F, release HP
Friendship (further than sweep): Run, LK, Run, Run, U
Babality: Run, Run, LK
Brutality: HP, Block, LK, LK, LK, HK, LP, LP, LP, HP, LP
Stage: Block, Block, HK
Standard Combo: LK, LK, HP, HP, D+HP

Kitana
Fan Lift: B, B, B, HP Fan
Throw: F, F, HP+LP
Square Wave Punch: D, B, HP
Fatality (close): Run, Run, Block, Block, LK
Fatality (close): B, D, F, F, HK
Animality (beyond sweep): D, D, D, D, Run
Friendship: D, B, F, F, LP
Babality: F, F, D, F, HK
Brutality: HP, HP, Block, HK, Block, LK, Block, LP, Block, HP, Block
Stage: F, D, D, LK
Standard Combo: HP, HP, B+LP, F+HP

Kung lao
Hat Throw: B, F, LP
Teleport: D, U
Flying Kick (in air): D, HK

Nintendo 64 A-Z of Cheats Volume 2

Spin: F, D, F, Run repeatedly
Fatality: Run, Block, Run, Block, D
Fatality (inside sweep): F, F, B, D, HP
Animality (close): Run, Run, Run, Run, Block
Friendship (outside sweep): Run, LP, R, LK
Babality: D, F, F, HP
Brutality: HP, LP, LK, HK, Block, HP, LP, LK, HK, Block, HP
Stage: D, D, F, F, LK
Standard Combo: HP, LP, HP, LP, LK, LK, B+HK

Liu kang
High Fireball: F, F, HP Low
Fireball: F, F, LP
Flying Kick: F, F, HK
Bicycle Kick: Hold LK then release
Fatality: F, F, D, D, LK
Fatality: U, D, U, U, Block+Run
Animality (sweep): D, D, U
Friendship: Run, Run, Run, D+Run
Babality: D, D, D, HK
Brutality: HP, LP, HP, Block, LK, HK, HK, LK, HK, LP, HP
Stage: Run, Block, Block, LK
Standard Combo: HP, HP, Block, LK, LK, HK, LK

Mileena
Sai Throw: Hold HP (3 seconds), then release
Warp Kick: F, F, LK
Roll: B, B, D, HK
Fatality (far): B, B, B, F, LK
Fatality (close): D, F, D, F, LP
Animality (close): F, D, D, F, HK
Friendship: D, D, B, F, HP
Babality: D, D, F, F, HP
Brutality: HP, LP, LP, HP, Block, HK, LK, LK, HK, Block, HP
Stage: D, D, D, LP
Standard Combo: HP, HP, HK, HK, U+LK, U+HK

Noob saib
Teleport and Throw: D, U
Two Noob Throw: F, F, HP
Disable Blocking Fireball: D, F, LP
Fatality (sweep): B, B, F, F, HK
Fatality (close): D, D, U, Run
Babality: F, F, F, LP
Friendship: F, F, B, HP
Animality (outside sweep): B, F, B, F, HK
Stage: F, D, F, Block
Brutality: HP, LK, LP, Block, LK, HK, HP, LP, Block, LK, HK
Standard Combo: LK, LK, LK, LK

Nightwolf
Arrow: D, B, LP
Red Arrow: Arrow move repeatedly
Hatchet Uppercut: D, F, HP
Shadow Shoulder: F, F, LK
Red Shadow Shoulder: B, B, F, HK
Glow (reflects projectiles): B, B, B, HK
Fatality (close): U, U, B, F, Block
Fatality (outside sweep): B, B, D, HP
Animality (close): F, F, D, D (wolf)
Friendship: (outside close): Run, Run, Run, D
Babality: F, B, F, B, LP
Brutality: HP, HP, HK, HK, Block, Block, LP, HP, HK
Stage: R, R, Block
Standard Combo: LK, HP, HP, LP, Hatchet, Hatchet

Rain
Lightning: B, B, HP
Levitation Ball: D, F, HP
Super Roundhouse: B+HK
Fatality (close): F, F, D+HP
Fatality (just outside sweep) D, D, B, F, HK
Friendship D, F, F, F, LP

Animality (close): Block, Block, Run, Run, Block
Babality: F, B, B, HP
Stage: F, D, F, LP
Brutality: HP, HP, Block, LK, HK, Block, LK, HK, Block, HP, LP
Standard Combo: HP, HP, LP, HP

Rayden
Lightning: D, F, LP
Reverse Lightning: D, B, LP
Teleport: D, U
Flying Torpedo: B, B, F
Fatality (close): Hold HP for 5 seconds, then release
Fatality (close): Hold BlockK, U, U, U, release BlockK, HP
Fatality (close): F, F, D, HP
Fatality (close): Hold LK for 3 seconds, release, Block+LK
Friendship: D, B, F, HK
Babality: D, D, U, HK
Animality (far): D, F, D, HK
Stage: D, D, D, HP
Brutality: HP, HP, LK, LK, LK, HK, LP, LP, LP, Block, Block
Standard Combo: HP, HP, LP, D+LP, Jump, Flying Torpedo

Reptile
Acid Spit: F, F, HP
Slow Force Ball: B, B, HP+LP
Fast Force Ball: F, F, HP+LP
Slide: B+LP+Block+LK
Invisibility: U, D, HK
Run Past and Elbow: B, F, LK
Fatality (jump distance): B, F, D, Block
Fatality (sweep): F, F, U, U, HK
Animality (close): D, D, D, U, HK
Friendship (close): D, F, F, B, HK
Babality: F, F, B, D, LK
Brutality: HP, Block, HK, HK, Block, HP, LP, LK, LK, Block, LP, HP
Stage: Block, R, Block, Block
Standard Combo: HP, HP, HK, B+HK

Scorpion
Spear: B, B, LP
Teleport: D, B, HP
Forward Teleport: D, F, HP
Air Throw (must be in air): Block
Fatality (just outside sweep): F, F, F, B, LP
Fatality (jump distance): D, D, U, HK
Fatality (close): F, F, D, U, Run
Animality (close): F, U, U, HK
Friendship (close): B, F, F, B, LK
Babality: D, B, B, F, HP
Brutality: HP, HP, Block, HK, HK, LK, HK, HP, HP, LP, HP
Stage: F, U, U, LP
Standard Combo: HK, HK, LK, LK

Sektor
Teleport+Uppercut: F, F, LK
Straight Missile: F, F, LP
Double Missile: B, B, F, LP
Heat Seeking Missile: F, D, B, HP
Fatality (sweep): LP, Run, Run, Block
Fatality (over half screen): F, F, F, B, Block
Animality (close): F, F, D, U
Friendship (half screen): Run, Run, Run, Run, D
Babality: B, D, D, D, HK
Brutality: HP, HP, BlockK, BlockK, HK, HK, LK, LK, LP, LP, HP
Stage: Run, Run, Run, D
Standard Combo: HP, HP, HK, HK, B+HK

Shang tsung
1 Fireball: B, B, HP
2 Fireballs: B, B, F, HP
3 Fireballs: B, B, F, F, HP
Volcanic Eruption: F, B, B, LK

Nintendo 64 A-Z of Cheats Volume 2

Shao khan
Hammer: F, B, B, HP
Fireball: F, D, F, LK
Charge: F, F, HP
Upward Charge: D, D, F, HK
Taunt: Hold Block, U, U, Run
Laugh: D, D, Run
Fatality (sweep): F, F, B, HP

Sheeva
Teleport Stomp: D, U
Ground Shake: B, D, B, HK
Fireball: D, F, HP
Fatality (close): F, D, D, F, LP
Fatality (close): Hold HK, B, F, F, release HK
Animality (close): Run, Block, Block, Block, Block
Friendship: Hold HP, F, F, D, F, release HP, HP
Babality: D, D, D, B, HK
Brutality: HP, LP, Block, LK, HK, Block, HK, LK, Block, LP, HP
Stage: D, F, D, F, LP
Standard Combo: HP, HP, LP, HK, HK, LK, B+HK

Smoke (human)
Smoke (human)
Spear: B, B, LP
Teleport Punch: D, B, HP
Throw (in air): Block
Fatality (sweep): Run, Block, Run, Run, HK
Fatality (outside sweep): F, F, B, Run
Animality (far): F, F, F, B, HK
Friendship: D, F, F, F, Run
Babality: D, B, B, F, Run
Brutality HP, LK, LK, HK, Block, Block, LP, LP, HP, HP, Block
Stage: F, U, U, LP
Standard Combo: HK, HK, LK, B+LK, B+HK

Smoke (cyber)
Harpoon: B, B, LP
Teleport+Uppercut: F, F, LK
Invisible: U, U, Run
Air Throw (in air): Block
Fatality (across screen): U, U, F, D
Fatality (sweep): Hold Run+Block, D, D, F, U, release
Animality (outside sweep): D, F, F, Block
Friendship (across screen): Run, Run, Run, HK
Babality: D, D, B, B, HK
Brutality HP, LK, LK, HK, Block, Block, LP, LP, HP, HP, Block, Block
Stage: F, F, D, LK
Standard Combo: HP, HP, LK, HK, LP

Sindel
Fireball: F, F, LP
Double Fireball: B, B, F, LP
Air Firebal: D, F, LK
Fly: B, B, F, HK (Block to land)
Scream: F, F, F, HP
Fatality (sweep): Run, Run, Block, Run, Block
Fatality (close): Run, Block, Block, Run+Block
Animality (anywhere): F, F, U, HP (wasp)
Friendship: Run, Run, Run, Run, Run, U
Babality: Run, Run, Run, U
Brutality: HP, Block, LK, Block, LK, HK, Block, HK, LK, Block, LP
Stage: D, D, D, LP
Standard Combo: HK, HP, HP, LP, HK

Sonya
Energy Rings: D, F, LP
Leg Grab: D+LP+Block
Square Wave Punch: F, B, HP
Bicycle Kick: B, B, D, HK
Fatality (over half screen): Hold Block+Run, U, U, B, D,

Nintendo 64 A-Z of Cheats Volume 2

release
Fatality: B, F, D, D, Run
Animality (close): Hold LP, B, F, D, F, release
Friendship: B, F, B, D, Run
Babality: D, D, F, LK
Brutality: HP, LK, Block, HP, LK, Block, HP, LP, Block, HK, LK
Stage: F, F, D, HP
Standard Combo: HK, HK, HP, HP, LP, B+HP

Stryker
Double High Grenade: B, D, F, HP
Double Low Grenade: B, D, F, LP
Shoot Gun: B, F, HP
High Grenade: D, B, HP
Low Grenade: D, B, LP
Baton Trip: F, B, LP
Baton Throw: F, F, HK
Fatality (close): D, F, D, F, Block
Fatality (just under full screen): F, F, F, LK
Animality (sweep): Run, Run, Run, Block
Friendship: LP, Run, Run, LP
Babality: D, F, F, B, HP
Brutality: HP, LP, HK, LK, HP, LP, LK, HK, HP, LK, LK
Stage: F, U, U, HK
Standard Combo: LK, HP, HP, LP

Morphs
Cyrax: Block, Block, Block
Ermac: D, D, U
Jade: F, F, D, D+Block
Jax: F, F, D, LP
Johnny Cage: F, D, F, HP
Kabal: LP, Block, HK
Kano: B, F, Block
Kitana: F, D, F, Run
Liu Kang: F, D, B, U, F

Mileena: Run, Block, HK
Nightwolf: U, U, U
Noob Saibot: F, D, D, B, HK
Rain: Run, Block, LK
Rayden: Block, Run, Block
Reptile: Run, Block, Block, HK
Scorpion: D, D, F, LP
Sektor: D, F, B, Run
Sheeva: F, D, F, LK, LK
Sindel: B, D, B, LK
Smoke (human): Block, Run, LK
Smoke (cyber): B, B, D, LK
Sonya: D+Run+LP+Block
Stryker: F, F, F, HK
Sub-Zero: Block, Block, Run, R

Sub zero

Freeze: D, F, LP
Ground Freeze: D, B, LK
Ice Shower: D, F, HP
Ice Shower (front): D, F, B, HP
Ice Shower (behind): D, B, F, HP
Ice Statue: D, B, LP
Slide: B+LP+Block+LK
Fatality (close): D, F, F, F, HP
Fatality (close): D, D, D, F, HP
Animality (close): B, B, F, D, HP
Friendship (close): D, B, B, F, LK
Babality: D, B, B, HK
Brutality: HP, LK, HK, LP, HP, HK, HK, HP, HP, LP
Stage: F, D, F, F, HP
Standard Combo: HP, HP, LK, B+HK, F+LK

MULTI RACING CHAMPIONSHIP

Guaranteed Victory
If you want to win every time, choose Kingroader (the yellow Jeep-type vehicle) and adjust the aerodynamics so that the maximum speed is 205kph. Assuming you aren't completely incompetent at driving, you'll hardly ever skid (even on snow), allowing you to out-pace even cars which should be much faster.

Doing this, you'll be able to unlock the hidden cars and mirror tracks even faster than you would otherwise, not that it should take more than a day anyway...

Hidden Route
The Downtown track has a hidden route, which can massively reduce your time and is a lot easier than the normal track. At the top of the hill that leads to the waterfall, there is a tree just before some fences. Drive through the tree (don't worry, it won't hurt!) and you'll be on easy street!

Quick Start
Hold down the A button at the beginning of the race when the countdown reaches '1'.

Downtown Track Shortcut
Drive on past the windmills and zig-zags uphill and look for the wide turn near the waterfall. There is a tree next to a one way sign on the right edge of the track. If you drive towards the tree you should find a gap in the fence that will lead you onto a dirt road. The road passes through the waterfall into a tunnel and you'll emerge close to the finish line.

MYSTICAL NINJA STARRING GOEMON

Fight Impact Bosses From Menu
Find every silver fortune doll in the game (you'll know if you've got them all because your life gauge will be full). At the end of the game, after the credits, a fortune doll count appears and a new option will be available on the options menu, allowing you to play against the four Impact robots in sequence.

NAGANO OLYMPIC HOCKEY '98

Continual Fighting
Make sure the 'Fighting' selection is highlighted on the options screen, hold L and press C Right, C Left, C Left, C Right, C Down, C Up, C Up, C Down, C Left, C Right, C Right, C Left, C Right, C Left.

Change Player Appearance
On the options screen press C Left + R, C Down + R or C Up + R. Adjust the first six bits of the 16-bit register to alter the game by pressing:

C-Down + R to alter bits 1 and 2
C-Left + R to alter bits 3 and 4
C-Up + R to alter bits 5 and 6

Register	Effect
100000	Squat players.
010000	Squat players, big heads.

Nintendo 64 A-Z of Cheats Volume 2

110000	Squat players, small heads.
001000	Squat players, small announcer's voice.
000100	Big players, big announcer's voice.
000010	Squat players, small announcer's voice.
000001	Stretched players, big announcer' voice.
110110	Big players, small heads.
010010	Squat players, big heads.
010101	Big players, big heads.
010001	Stretched players, big heads.

NBA HANGTIME

Duplicate Players

If you've bought this annoying basketball game, you might decide that your day would be made if you could have two Dennis Rodmans (Rodmen?) on your team. Now you can. Enter any of the following codes as your name and use the PIN 0000 to access them.

Ahrdwy	(Penny Hardaway)
Cliffr	(Cliff Robinson)
Davidr	(David Robinson)
Dream	(Hakeem Olajuwon)
Elliot	(Sean Elliot)
Ewing	(Patrick Ewing)
Glennr	(Glenn Robinson)
Ghill	(Grant Hill)
Hgrant	(Horace Grant)
Johnson	(Larry Johnson)
Kemp	(Shawn Kemp)
Kidd	(Jason Kidd)
Malone	(Karl Malone)
Miller	(Reggie Miller)
Motumb	(Dikembe Mutumbo)
Mourng	(Alonzo Mourning)

Mursan	(Gheorghe Muresan)
Pippen	(Scottie Pippen)
Rodman	(Dennis Rodman)
Rice	(Glen Rice)
Smits	(Rik Smits)
Stackh	(Jerry Stackhouse)
Starks	(John Starks)
Webb	(Spud Webb)
Webber	(Chris Webber)

NBA IN THE ZONE '98

Easy Free Throws

To make this rather difficult activity a tad easier, repeatedly push the analogue stick upwards when you're about to take the throw, and the shot indicator will slow down.

NFL QUARTERBACK CLUB 98

Cheat Mode

Enter the following codes on the cheat menu screen for the desired result. Correct code entry will be confirmed by a tone (hi, Tone!).

EFFECT	CODE
Eight downs	8DWNDRV
Tall, thin players	BBMNTBL
Expert defence	BGBFYDF
Strong receivers	BGBFYFF
Longer dives	BGSPRDV
Spinning receiver	BGTWSTRS
Top quarterback	BRDWYNMTH
Longer jumps	CRLLWYS

Nintendo 64 A-Z of Cheats Volume 2

Slow motion	FRMBYFRM
Fumble mode	GTNHNDS
Repeated fumbles	GTNHNDS
Short players	JPNSMWR
Instant passing	LDSTRTRK
Disable cheats	LLCHTSFF
Lousy defence	LLDFSCK
Lousy offence	LLFFSCK
Ball tipped when passing	LWYSTPSS
Repeated dives	MNFLDMD
No tackles	NBCTCKLS
Crawling players	PBYBYMD
Lousy players	PWHYRMN
Sledge mode	SNWSLDS
100-yard passes	SPRBGRMS
Always tackle	SPRDPRTCKL
Expert players	SPRTMMD
Speedy running	SPRTRBMD
Acclaim and Iguana teams	STNTXTM
No fumbles	TGHTGRP
Lousy quarterback	TRNTDLFR
Electric football mode	YLCTRCFB
Max discipline	YNSTYNS

NHL BREAKAWAY '98

Cheat Menu

To bring up the cheat menu, bring up the main menu and press C Left, C Right, C Left, C Right, R, R. If you've done it correctly, the cheat menu option will appear. From the cheat menu, you'll be able to change the player type and size for both teams, change the ref size, access a sound test menu, change the house rules, enable big checking, increase the likelyhood of the rink glass shattering, and increase the chances of equipment being lost.

Player Inspection
On the player creation screen, you can view your player by pressing C Up, C Down, C Left, or C Right to rotate the player in any dimension.

Remove Opposing Goalie
Press Start during play and select the game options menu followed by the game settings menu. Select the 'Controller Set-up' option and move your controller across so that you're commanding the other team. Select the 'Pull Goalie' option from 'Team Options' and use 'Controller Set-up' again to switch the teams back and resume the game, leaving the CPU's goal untended!
Alternatively, if you're losing really badly, just select 'Controller Set-up' and switch teams for good.

Bonus Teams
Press C Left, R, R, L, L, C Right on the main menu and you'll be able to access extra teams.

Perfect Players
Go to the Create Player screen and give your name as 'Jim Hung'. You'll then be able to change any player characteristic, and create some super athletes!

100 Bonus Points
On the main season menu enter the following code: C Left, C Left, C Right, C Right, C Left, C Left, C Right, C Right and R to add 100 bonus points. You can do this as many times as you want.

OFF-ROAD CHALLENGE

Punisher Truck
Push C Down on the vehicle selection screen.

Nintendo 64 A-Z of Cheats Volume 2

4x4 Monster Truck
Push C Up on the vehicle selection screen.

Thunderbolt Truck
Push C Left on the vehicle selection screen.

Crusher Truck
Push C Right on the vehicle selection screen.

Secret Tracks
There are three hidden tracks in the game, although they're not that different to the normal ones! Here's how you access them.

Flagstaff
On the track select screen, hold Left, L and Z as you select the Mojave track.

El Cajon
On the track sleect screen, hold Up, L, R and Z as you select the El Paso track.

Guadalupe
On the track select screen, hold Down, R and Z as you select the Las Vegas track.

PUYO PUYO SUN 64 (IMPORT)

Select Opponent's Character (Two-player mode)
On the character select screen, highlight Doraco (the first – leftmost –character on the front row) and hold Start for three seconds. The one- and two-player selectors will now switch, so you can make your opponent play as someone they really hate. Pointless but fun.

Play As Carbuncle
On the character select screen, highlight Arle (the second character on the front row) and hold Start for three seconds. Carbuncle, the little dancing rabbit thing who appears throughout the game, can now be selected.

Play As Satan
On the character select screen, highlight Shezo (the third character on the front row) and hold Start for three seconds. Satan will make herself (yes, herself) known. If this game gets a Western release, what are the odds on her name changing?

Random Character Select
On the character select screen, highlight Rulue (the fourth character on the front row) and hold Start for three seconds. You will now play as a randomly chosen character.

Elephant Mode
On the character select screen, highlight Elephant (the, erm, elephant) and hold Start for three seconds. All the characters will turn into prehensile-schnozzed pachyderms!

QUAKE 64

Super Cheat
Enter QQQQ QQQQ QQQQ QQQQ as a password. You'll get an "Invalid Password" message. A 'Debug' selection will appears on the option menu. From here you'll be able to access level select, invincibility, all weapons and targeting.

No Clipping Mode
Enter NOCLIP as a password.

QUEST 64

Super Attack
During combat, move so that your staff is within striking

distance, then select any spell and press A to launch an attack with both staff and spell in only one turn.

RAMPAGE WORLD TOUR

Alternate Coloured Characters
Go to the character selection screen and highlight George, Ralph, or Lizzy. Before you select them, you'll be able to change their colour by pressing up on the d-pad. Each monster comes in a range of tasteful hues just perfect for those all-important international wrecking sprees!

Play As VERN
To play as the Violent Enraged Radioactive Nemesis, eat the canisters of Toxic Waste that you'll find somewhere near the Scum Labs buildings. For the rest of the level you'll be super-strong, have the ability of flight, and be able to shoot fireballs with the C Down button.

Hidden Cities
To get to the hidden cities, repeatedly punch the sign that switches between pictures of various landscapes and then tap one of the following buttons while on the screen that shows your next destination.
George: Press the jump button
Lizzie: Press the punch button
Ralph: Press the kick button
Not every destination has a hidden city, so you'll just have to experiment!

ROBOTRON

The following codes should all be entered whilst on the Robotron game setup menu screen.

Level Select
Down, Up, C Left, Down, C Left, C Right, Down, C Right.

50 Lives
Up, Up, Down, Down, Left, Right, Left, Right, C Left, C Right, C Left, C Right.

Game Boy Mode
Up, Down, Right, C Left, Down, Up, Left, C Right, Up, Down.

The following codes need to be entered while playing the game.

Speed Up
During the game, Left, Left, Right, Right, C Up.

Shield
During the game, Down, Left, C Left, C Right.

Flame Thrower
During the game, Down, Right, Down, Right, C Right.

Gas Gun
During the game, Up, Down, C Right, C Left.

Four-Way Fire
During the game Down, Down, Up, C Right.

Three-Way Fire
During the game, Right, Right, C Left, C Down.

Two-Way Fire
During the game, Up, C Up, Up, C Up.

Nintendo 64 A-Z of Cheats Volume 2

Extra lives
Enter the following passwords to start the game with 110 lives.

Easy difficulty level: BSBBBBTJBB
Normal difficulty level: BCBBLBTJBB
Insane difficulty level: BFBBBCTJBB

Passwords
Level 90: CSSRQQHLRH
Level 98: DGQDQQLLHJ
Level 99: DNKFQGLLJJ
Level 100: DDJGQGJLLJ
Level 101: DLRHQQDLMJ
Level 102: DBBJQLDLNS
Level 103: DNMJQGFLPS
Level 104: DNTJQLCLQJ
Level 105: DGBKQLCLRJ

Access Final Level
Enter BJTCNGLFCR as a password.

SAN FRANSCISCO RUSH

Race As Taxi
Collect at least half the keys hidden on any track. The cab can only be selected on the same track from which it was unlocked.

Race As Hot Rod
Collect all of the keys hidden on any track. The Hot Rod can only be selected on the same track from which it was unlocked.

Race As Formula 1 Car
Complete all 24 races in Circuit mode then press Z, Z, Z, Z on the track selection screen. A horn will confirm correct code entry.

Race As Mine
Press C Right, C Right, Z, C Down, C Up, Z, C Left, C Left on the car selection screen.

Mines
Press L, R, L, R, L, R on the setup screen. Traffic cones will turn into explosive mines.

Inverted Tracks
Press Up, Right, Down, Left, Down, Right, Up, Left on the setup screen.

Disable Stuck Car Help
Press C Up, C Up, C Up, C Up on the setup screen. The number "00.06" will appear to confirm correct code entry. This will mean that you won't be moved back onto the track if you stay in one place too long (useful when searching for keys).

Toggle Car Size
Hold C Down and press C Up on the car selection screen. Release both buttons, hold C Up and press C Down. The car in the on-screen window will change size if you've done it correctly. Repeat to cycle through the different car sizes.

Toggle Rear Tyre Size
Hold C Right and press C Left on the car selection screen. Release both buttons, hold C Left and press C Right. The tyres on the car in the on-screen window will change if you've done it correctly. Repeat to cycle through the different tyre sizes.

Toggle Front Tyre Size
Hold C Left and press C Right on the car selection screen. Release both buttons, hold C Right and press C Left. The tyres on the car in the on-screen window will change if you've done it correctly. Repeat to cycle through the different tyre sizes.

Nintendo 64 A-Z of Cheats Volume 2

Alternate Fog Colour
Hold Z and press C Down, C Down, C Down on the car selection screen. The colour of the fog in the on-screen window will change if you've done it correctly. Repeat to cycle through the various colours.

Toggle Gravity
Hold Z and press Up, Down on the setup screen. Release Z and press Up, Down, Up, Down. An icon will appear on-screen to confirm correct code entry. Repeat to cycle through the other gravity settings.

Toggle Road Textures
Hold C Right and press L on the setup screen. Release both buttons and press Z. Hold C Right and press L. Release both buttons and press Z. A checkered flag will appear on-screen to confirm correct code entry. Repeat to cycle through the textures.

Toggle Camera Height And Distance
Hold L and press Up or Down during the game.

Toggle Collision Damage
Press Left, hold Right and press C Right on the setup screen. Release both buttons and press C Up, C Left, C Down, Z. The icon of a bus will appear on- screen to confirm correct code entry.

Random High Scores
Press L, R, L, R, L, R, L, R while the "Fast Times" or "Best Laps" information is displayed on the records screen to give any blank entries random names and scores.

Crashed Car Replay
Crash as you pass the finish line then hold L & R & Z while the words "Game Over" are flashing until the high score screen appears. In the replay your car will be a smoking wreck!

Drive Crashed Car
Hold C Up and press Z, Z, Z, Z on the car selection screen. Repeat to toggle between two different crashes.

Resume Race From Site Of Crash
Hold Z & C Left & C Right on the setup screen. Release the C buttons and hold C Right and C left. Release all the buttons. An "R' will appear to confirm correct code entry.

Special Car In Circuit Mode
Win a circuit, select the same player again and press Z, Z, Z, Z on the track selection screen to access the special car.

Toggle Race Clock
Hold Z & C Down & C Up on the setup screen. Release C Down and C Up. Hold C Up & C Down. A clock icon will appear to confirm correct code entry.

Switch Control Directions
Highlight "Mirror" on the options screen. Hold down all the C buttons and press Left or Right to access the "Extreme" option.

Tag Mode
Abort the race during countdown at the beginning of a two player practice game. Both timers will start at five minutes and the timer of the player who is "it" will start. To stop their timer and start their opponent's, the "it" player must "tag" them by making contact with them.

Change Screen Position
Hold L & R and move the analogue stick to adjust the screen.

Foggy Night
Set the "Fog" option to "Heavy" on the options screen. Hold all the C buttons and press Right to activate foggy night mode.

Track one

Key 1
Turn around at the start line and drive down the tunnel. The key is on the left at the very end of the tunnel.

Key 2
Travel along from the start until you reach the bridge. Drive about halfway along and turn around, then accelerate back the way you came, keeping to the right. As you leave the bridge, bear right onto the sand. You should be able to see the key (just), so aim at it, and if you are travelling fast enough a small bump will launch you into the air to collect the key

Key 3
From key 2, travel over the bridge, keeping your speed somewhere between 120 and 140mph. As you pass through the first checkpoint, aim to the left, which should take you up a small hill. The hill will launch you into the air towards the key.

Key 4
Travel on up the track from key 3 and as you reach checkpoint two, aim left to go off the track and break through the fence. Follow the path until it passes around a small hill, and go up it. The key is on the top of the hill.

Key 5
Make your way through the fourth checkpoint (also the finish line) and follow the road around. As you come off the bend, near the fifth checkpoint, there is a path to the left. Take this path and you will come to a tunnel, to the right of which is the key.

Key 6
Take the tunnel from key 5, which will bring you out near the finish line. As soon as you leave the tunnel, bear hard left and keep on the grass by the wall. Keep hugging the wall and you'll move onto a grassy ledge, which if followed will take you to key 6...

Track two

Key 1
Make your way to the third checkpoint, then keep to the left (through the cones) and accelerate towards the gap in the overpass. If your speed is correct, you'll land on the lower part of the overpass, although if you go too fast you may collide with the upper overpass. One on the lower level, drive to the end where you'll find a red half-pipe, and bear right. There is a ledge on the left-hand wall (as you enter the pipe) which contains the key, and all you've got to do is drive up to it.

Key 2
Still in the red half-pipe, at the far end you'll notice a section which forms a loop. The key is in the middle of the loop at the top. To get the key, accelerate at full speed up the side of the loop so that you cling to the inside. If you miss the key, simply keep the power on and you'll go down one side and back up the other for another pass.

Key 3
Return to the third checkpoint, and make your way along the road on the left to the gap in the overpass again. This time, drive very slowly (only a few miles per hour) so that when you reach the edge you drop down to the level below. Turn around, and drive back the way you came on the level above, and you'll find the key.

Key 4
From key 3, make your way to the fourth checkpoint. Follow the road up the hill, and then at the top when the road turns right, aim at full speed directly for the trailer of the truck in front of you. You'll pass under the truck, get boosted into the air, and should land on the roof of a building. Follow the roof (the yellow and black chevrons will guide your way) until you come to a yellow and black ramp. Drive slowly up to the ramp, move past it just to the left and drop down. You will find the next key here.

Key 5
Return to the bend with the trailer you went under for key 4. This time, follow the road down the hill and aim for the pond on the left, keeping your speed somewhere between 80 and 100 mph. If you've judged it correctly, you should bounce off the pond and into a hidden tunnel in the building opposite. The key is here.

Key 6
Back slowly out of the tunnel where you found key 5, and drop down by the pond. Turn around so you're facing back up the hill. In front of you is a path that leads to the left. Follow it to a short tunnel, at the end of which is the key.

Key 7
From key 6, go through checkpoint five, keeping an eye out on the left for another pond. When you see it, approach it and slowly drive into it; you'll drop to the bottom and find the key.

Track three
Key 1
Make your way from the start line to the first turn. Keep to the left and you should find a row of five trees. Just past the trees is a flight of stairs. Go up these slowly and turn left at the top to find the key.

Key 2
Now race to the third checkpoint and reverse your direction. Accelerate as fast as possible, following the road and keeping to the middle. A short distance before the second checkpoint, the road rises sharply and this will catapult you into the air, allowing you to collect the key floating above the checkpoint.

Key 3
After key 2, return to the third checkpoint and bear left as the road turns right, taking you onto the grass. Aim between the two buildings to get onto the dirt track, and you'll find the key on the bend at the top of the first right-hand curve.

Key 4

Make your way to the fourth checkpoint, and go down the hill to the bottom. Then turn around and – keeping in the middle of the road – accelerate at full speed back up the hill. As you enter the tunnel, you should take off, collecting the key which is floating near the ceiling in the centre of the tunnel.

Key 5

Continue on to the sixth checkpoint, and at the hard-right turn just past it, keep left so that you pass into a narrow alley which goes up a hill. Follow the alley and you will find the key.

Key 6

Return to the sixth checkpoint, and then make your way towards the seventh. The track goes up a hill, curving to the left, and then again up another hill, also to the left. At the top of this second hill, if you bear hard-right you will find a wooden fence. Go through the gap in the right-hand end of the fence and then turn left to enter a narrow tunnel which leads to a room decorated in sky blue (literally). The key is just to the right as you enter the room.

Key 7

Make your way to the eighth checkpoint, and race down the hill from there, keeping to the left. At the first square flat area, steer hard left, and you will take off and fly across onto a small ledge, where you will find the next key.

Key 8

Drop off the ledge where you found key 7, and make your way towards the ninth checkpoint (which is also the finish line). Just before you pass the last checkpoint, turn left and aim to the right of the tram car for the last key.

Track four

Key 1

Go left from the start line towards the buses. Drive past the second bus and get in the right hand lane, accelerating until you hit a grass bank which will launch you into the air, throwing you towards the floating key.

Key 2
From the grassy bank where you found key 1, drive back towards the start and drop into the small concrete plaza. Accelerate at full speed towards the pool of water in the centre, which will catapult you into the air when you hit it, throwing you past the buses and into the fenced-off area containing the key.

Key 3
From the start again, follow the road along until it curves to the left twice. You should see a building with yellow and black arrows on it pointing to the left. Once around this, the next building in front of you has large arched windows. Instead of going left, head to the right of this building, onto the orange brick path, and follow this path along, round to the left and up to the green ramp. Hit the ramp at about 90mph, and you will land on a pathway, which if you follow it will take you to the roof of a building for the key.

Key 4
Do exactly what you did for key 3, except this time hit the green ramp at at least 100mph to launch you onto a different pathway, slightly above the first, which also contains a key.

Key 5
Make your way to the first checkpoint. As you pass through it, you'll notice a building with square white columns on your left. Go left at the end of this building. Then go right after the blue building on the right, and left at the dead end with the yellow and black indicator arrows. Very soon, you'll see a building on the right with blue windows. At the far end of this building is an alley, which you should turn down and follow for the key.

Key 6
Continue along the track until you reach the second checkpoint, then follow the road as it curves around three left curves. After

the third curve, slow a little and get into the far left hand lane (staying on the road). Soon you will find yourself on a raised pedestrian walkway. Follow this walkway, which will go hard left twice, until it leads you to a garage. At the end of the garage is the key.

Key 7
From key 6, head towards the third checkpoint. Before you reach the third checkpoint, you'll see a black and yellow ramp on the grass to the right. Drive onto the grass, and take the tunnel to the right of the ramp, driving at just below 100mph. You'll take off and land near another ramp. A narrow pathway just to the right of this ramp which leads to the key.

Key 8
Head past the third checkpoint and make your way along the road towards the finish. The road will fork right and left and join up, then fork again. At the second fork, go left, and on the left you will see a row of parking meters. Not far along this row is the entrance to a narrow allow, which if you follow it will take you to the final key.°

Track five

Key 1
From the start, follow the road along and left, then take the first right and the first left. The road will go on for a bit, until it turns sharp right, followed by sharp left – you should pass the 'Wrongway' building just off the road on the left, and see two yellow and black arrows straight in front of you. Aim between the arrows, and drive fairly slowly until you go up a small green ramp and onto a road. Turn left and head along the road, turning right at the corner. You'll shortly come to a purple building on the left, where you need to turn sharp right and head across the road onto a narrow pathway between two buildings. The key is here.

Key 2
Return to the start line, and repeat the steps it took to get to the

gap between the yellow and black arrows. Go between the signs again, and this time keep left and accelerate so that when you reach the green ramp you take off. Your car should fly across to another ramp on top of a building, then bounce off that ramp onto the building with the key.

Key 3
Head for the second checkpoint after picking up key 2. Shortly before you get to the second checkpoint, the road divides into two. Just before the fork, get onto the left pavement, and accelerate. You'll hit a ramp which will launch you into the air at the buildings in front of you. You need to aim to the right to land on top of the smaller white building where you will find the key.

Key 4
Carry on from key 3 towards the second checkpoint, taking the left-hand fork when the road splits. As the road rejoins, you'll see the checkpoint on your right. Instead of turning right for the checkpoint, carry straight on down the hill and you'll see a petrol station on the right at the next corner. Veer right and turn into the station for the key.

Key 5
Go through the second checkpoint, head all the way up the hill to the corner and turn left. After the first downward slope, turn around 180° and veer right into the tunnel. Blast along the tunnel and you should pass over the pit with the spikes in it to see a ramp. Aim to the right of the ramp for the key.

Key 6
From key 5, go back through the tunnel, down another downward slope and onto a third slope. On the right of the third slope, you'll see two buildings, one brown and one blue, with a gap in between them. Drive into this gap and turn right into an underground garage for the key.

Key 7

Carry on down the hill and past the start line. You should see a yellow and black arrow in front of you, and you need to drive around it to the right. Keep accelerating, and aim straight for the gates in front of you, taking you into the park. Follow the path through the park and then onto the grass and you'll find yourself heading for a fence. Crash through the fence, then double back and travel until you reach the beach. On the beach turn around, and accelerate back towards the beach ramp which will throw you onto the roof of the first building. You'll bounce from roof to roof until you reach the building with the key.

Key 8
Return to the beach, and once again accelerate towards the beach ramp, but this time aim to the right so that you fly across to the white-roofed building on a pier. The key is at the far end of the pier.

Track Six

Key 1
Make your way to the first checkpoint, and get in the left-hand lane on the left carriageway. A short way along the road you'll see some trees on the left, followed by a grey wall set slightly back from the track, with a small gap blocked by a fence. Go through the fence and into the cave beyond for the key.

Key 2
Continue along the track until you pass the second checkpoint. Once you've crossed the grey bridge, come left off the road and onto the grass by the lake, and follow the waterline until you come to the next key which is by a small slope.
Key 3
Now make your way back to the start line, and immediately past it, turn right, then turn left and go up a steep hill. Follow the road straight on after the top of the hill, and you'll come onto a dirt track. Keep going until you come off the dirt track, and you'll see a building on the right. Keep on the road and drive past the front of

Nintendo 64 A-Z of Cheats Volume 2

the building, and you should see a path on the right leading into the place through two pillars. The key is behind the pillar on the left as you go in.

Key 4
From key 3, carry on along the road and you'll come to the third checkpoint. Turn right just after the checkpoint into a car park behind some buildings. The key is on some grass behind a building in the far left hand corner.

Key 5
Come out of the car park and turn back through the checkpoint, so that you're going in the opposite direction. Make sure you're travelling slowly, and go sharp right just past the checkpoint, taking you down a steep grass bank. Just before you reach the water, turn right and you'll come to a tunnel which leads to the secret stunt area.
 Go down the tunnel, and drive towards the far-left of the cave. You will climb the wall, and if you've going the right speed (around 85mph) you should land on a shelf in the wall. Drive into the ring for the key.

Key 6
Still in the secret stunt area, drive around the wall to the right, again at around 85mph. When you see the loop, aim for the grey bit directly in front of it to ramp up through the loop for the key.

Key 7
Getting out of the secret stunt area is a bit of a pain, so it's easier to restart the race. From the start, turn 180° and head immediately right, then left, and up the steep hill. At the first junction, turn left which takes you down a hill, then veer right onto the grey bit at the side of the road, keeping your speed down, and travel down the grass bank and to the right, taking you behind a building where the key is hidden in a little alcove.

Key 8
Return to the top of the hill where you turned left for key 7, and turn left again, this time accelerating to pick up speed, and

aiming at the grey bit on the right again. Hit this fast enough and you'll take off and fly to the key which is on a little island.

Access Secret Track

To begin with you need to have completed a circuit and have it stored in memory. If you haven't done this yet and want to speed things up, then try entering the following winning circuit code:
8DP5KG5L4G59P
G92WVCQY0DRDQ

Apparently one or two versions of the game may not accept the above code, in which case use this one instead:
9DQ6LH6M5H6$Q
H$3XWCR01DTDR

Once you've entered the code, finish the circuit. You then need to use the A and B buttons to move between selection screens.

1. On car selection screen: Hold C Left, press Z, release both and press Left.
2. On setup screen: Hold C Up, press Z, release both and press Up
3. On track selection screen: Hold C Right, press Z, release both and press Right
4. On car selection screen: Hold C Down, press Z, release both and press Down, L, R
5. Go to the track selection screen and choose track seven. Woohoo!

SHADOWS OF THE EMPIRE

For these cheats to work the game has to be on Medium level. You'll need a Controller Pak to save your game – assuming you have one, start a new save slot and call it .Wampa..Stompa (each . represents a space). You must get the case of the letters correct for the cheat to work. When you start the game, pause it, go to the options menu and set the controller type to 'traditional'. Now you can play as the forces of evil!

Play As AT-ST
In the second round of the Hoth battle, when the Scout Walkers appear press Left on the D-Pad and C Right simultaneously, then push Up. The C Right button will then let you change camera views until you see the AT-ST. Now use the D-Pad to stomp some Rebel ass!

Play As Wampa
On the 'Escape From Echo Base' level, repeat the above code and press C Right until the Wampa appears. As with the AT-ST, the D-Pad is used to control the new character – push Down to attack.

Play As Stormtrooper
Repeat the code to access the Wampa, but keep pushing C Right until the stormtrooper appears.

Play As TIE Fighter
This requires you to collect all the Challenge Points on the Medium skill level. Once you reach the Skyhook battle, hold C Right for five seconds to turn the Outrider into an X-Wing. Cool enough, but if you hold C Right for another five seconds, you will now be flying a TIE Fighter!

End Sequence
End your name as _Credits (a space before the first C). When you begin the game, you will be taken to the end sequence.

Cheats Menu
This code grants you access to a multitude of menu options, namely all weapons and items, invincibility, 50 lives, sleeping

villains, kill Dash (?), teleport, level select, walk through walls and unlock all levels. Here's how it works.

1. As usual use a game with the player's name as ".Wampa..Stompa". The name must be written correctly, including capitalisation, with ONE space before Wampa and TWO spaces between Wampa and Stompa.
2. Begin playing on any level and pause the game.
3. Hold down all of the following buttons: All the C buttons, Z, L, R and d-pad Left.
4. While holding all the above buttons down, move the analogue stick halfway to the left (using your chin or someone else's help), and hold it until you hear a sound.
5. Release all the buttons, press them again, and this time hold the analogue stick halfway to the right, waiting until you hear the sound.
6. Repeat this process again with the analogue stick to the left, then again to the right, and then again to the left.
7. Pink text should appear at the top of the screen. Use L and R to change the options – some of them can be changed by pushing the control stick up and down. Press A to activate them.
8. To get the cheat menu back, pause the game, then hold down all the buttons used in Step 3 above and move the analogue stick left or right.
This also enables an option marker in yellow on the pause menu which gives you access to game secrets for each level.

SNOWBOARD KIDS

Turbo Start
Tap A repeatedly when the 'Ready' message appears at the start and your kid will jump out into an early lead without needing to build up speed.

All Characters, Boards And Courses
From the start screen, enter Analogue stick Down, Analogue

stick Up, D-pad Down, D-pad Up, C Down, C Up, L, R, Z, D-pad Left, C right, Analogue stick Up, B, D-pad Right, C Left.

Quicksand Valley
Get gold on courses one to six. A new snowboard and the Quicksand Valley desert track will now be available.

Access Silver Mountain
Get gold on Quicksand Valley.

Access Ninja Land
Get gold on Silver Mountain.

Play As Ninja
Get gold on Ninja Land.

TETRISPHERE

Go to the 'new name' option, and press L, C Right and C Down to bring up some weird characters. Then enter the following names for extra spherical action!

Lines Game
Enter the name LINES to play the Lines game. You have to drag the blocks into rows and columns, rather than stacking them, to make them disappear.

Access All Levels
To play the level of your choosing without having to spin through the whole game, enter the <Saturn> <Spaceship> <Rocket> <Heart> <Skull> characters. You will now find a level select when you open a previously saved game.

New Music
Enter G<Alien Head>MEBOY to get some Game Boy-style new tunes.

View Credits
Work yourself into a fever pitch of excitement entering the name CREDITS to, shockingly, view the credits!

Vortex Strangeness
Another one of those weird little things that aren't exactly cheats, but still provide some amusement. First of all, go to the 'new name' option, and press L, C Right and C Down to bring up some weird characters. Then enter the name VORTEX, and press and hold the N64's reset button for four seconds to see a cut-scene of the game's robots being sucked into... a vortex!

TOP GEAR RALLY

PlayStation Mode
In technical terms, this cheat removes bi-linear filtering. If you're not a techno-ponce, it takes off the blurring and makes everything look horrible and blocky! During a game, press B, Left. Right, Up, Left, Z, Right for a ticket to Blocksville.

Acid Mode
Wow, far out, man! This strange code lets you see what it's like to drive while out of your head on illegal substances. During play, push C Down, Z, B, Up, Up, Right for that full-on hippy vibe.

All Tracks
The cheat to access all tracks we printed last issue does work – honest! To get it to work, you have to be on the title screen, since pressing A will put you onto the selection screen. Rest assured, you can play the Strip Mine track, and here are the pictures to prove it!

When the Kemco logo appears, quickly press A, Left, Left, Right, Down, Z – you'll then be able to play the Strip Mine track (and any others you haven't already opened) in Arcade and Time Attack modes.

Nintendo 64 A-Z of Cheats Volume 2

View Strip Mine
If you don't want to cheat your way to it, but still want a sneak preview, you can see a tour of the Strip Mine track during the credits by going to the credits icon in the options menu and pressing Left, C Down, Right, Down and Z.

Beachball Car
Enter B, B, A, Left, Left, C Down, A, Right on the Arcade mode-selection screen.

Cupra (Ice Cube) Car
Enter C Down, Up, B, Right, A, C Down, A, Right on the Arcade mode-selection screen.

Helmet Car (or Mini)
Enter Up, Up, Z, B, A, Left, Left on the Arcade mode-selection screen.

Bonus Cars
Complete the following seasons to access displayed cars:

No	Car
2	Type CE (Toyota Celica) and Type IP (Isuzu P)
3	Type M3 (BMW M3) and Type SP (Toyota Supra)
4	Type NS (Nissan Skyline) and Type RS (Ford RS 200)
5	Type PS (Porsche 959)

Change Car Colours
Can't be bothered to repaint your vehicle? Then hold down L, R and all four C buttons on the car select screen, then move the d-pad up or down. Once you've done that, you can change the car's colours by holding the L and R buttons and up or down on the d-pad, then pressing any of the C buttons.

TUROK DINOSAUR HUNTER

Full cheats list!
Enter the following in the cheat menu helpfully provided in the game.

DNCHN – Dana mode, gives you tiny enemies.
DLKTDR – Pen and Ink mode, turns everything into sketches.
SNFFRR – Disco mode – you figure it out!
THBST – Gallery mode – lets you view all the characters.
CMGTSMMGGTS – All weapons.
BLLTSRRFRND – Infinite ammo
FRTHSTHTTRLSCK – Unlimited lives.
THSSLKSCL – Spirit mode all the time.
GRGCHN – Greg mode – loads of weird stuff!
FDTHMGS – Credits.
RBNSMTH – Robin mode, infinite everything, invincibility.
CLLTHTNMTN – Quack Mode (Quake mickey-take).
NSTHMNDNT – Show Enemies.
LLTHCLRSFTHRNB – Weird Colours
NTHGTHDGDCRTDTRK – Weapons, invincibility, level warps, infinite ammo, big heads, the lot!

View Ending
Enter the everything code, turn on the invincibility option (always handy) and warp to the Campaigner. Sort him out and the ending is yours for the watching, for as long as it lasts (not long).

WAVE RACE 64

Different Coloured Jetskis
On the jetski selection screen, press Up on the analogue stick to change the colour and A to select it.

Ride the Dolphin
In the Stunt Mode, choose to visit Dolphin Park and ride the rings using the following special moves:

Handstand Backwards
Riding Standing
Somersault
Single Flip
Dive
Sideways Roll (in both directions)

If you do all these in the correct order, the dolphin will squeak. Now go to the Championship mode, normal and warm up, and press Down on the analogue stick and press A to get the dolphin.

WAR GODS

Access Cheat Menu
Want a whole host of extra options on Midway's new beat-'em-up? When you're on the initial War Gods title screen, before the game options appear, just press D-Pad right three times, B, B, A, A. If you've got it right, a voice will boom out to inform you of your success.

Easy Fatalities
Once the cheat mode is active, to make killing a whole lot easier press A, B and the Top and Right C buttons simultaneously after defeating your adversary.

Play As Exor
On the character selection screen, push L, D, D, R, L, U, L, U, R, D on either the D-pad or the analogue stick, then select any character. You will play the round as Exor.

Play As Grox
On the character selection screen, push D, R, L, L, U, D, R, U, L, L on either the D-pad or the analogue stick, then select any character. You will play the round as Grox.

WAYNE GRETZKY'S 3D HOCKEY

Hot new teams
Select Set-up right from the main menu and in the options screen, hold down the Left shoulder button and press the following Yellow buttons: Right, Left, Left, Right, Left, Left, Right, Left and Left. A 16 digit code will appear and four new teams will now be available.

Alter player sizes
In the options screen, press and hold the Yellow top button and press the Right shoulder button to display a 16 digit code. Change the digits using the Yellow buttons and you will alter the legs, bodies and heads of all subsequent players.

Invisible Players
Pause the game during the face off and select the Replay mode. Use the Left shoulder button to choose a team member, and then press the Right Shoulder button to select an opponent. When flashing, press Z and they will turn invisible.

WAYNE GRETZKY'S 3D HOCKEY 98

Old Teams
To play with some older teams, hold down L on the Options screen and (without releasing L) enter the following code: C Right, C Left, C Left, C Right, C Left, C Left, C Right, C Left, C Left.

Debug Mode
Teach yourself programming! Or not. You can play with the appearance of the hockey players using a 16-bit register. Modify the first six bits of the register by using the following button combinations.

C Down + R – alters bits 1 and 2
C Left + R – alters bits 3 and 4
C Up + R – alters bits 5 and 6

Register	Effect
100000	Gives you wide players.
010000	Gives you wide players with big heads.
110000	Gives you wide players with small heads.
001000	Gives you small players.
000100	Gives you tall players.
000010	Gives you small players.
000001	Gives you thin players.
110110	Gives you tall players with small heads.
010010	Gives you small players with large heads.
010101	Gives you tall players with large heads.
010001	Gives you thin players with large heads.

WCW VS NWO: WORLD TOUR

Play As Dallas Page
Choose WCW in the League Challenge and play through till you reach Dallas Page. Once you've successfully defeated him he will be available on the select screen.

Play As Glacier
Also in League Challenge mode, if you beat IU you'll then be able to access that frosty wrestler Glacier.

Play As Randy Savage
If the Macho Man is more your cup of tea, beat NWO and you'll be able to play as Randy Savage himself!

Play As Wrath
The character of Wrath can be gained by playing as DOA and beating him in single-player mode. Then he'll be yours to wreak havoc with.

A new game mode entitled 'Whole World Wrestling' will be available once you've successfully completed the other modes. Within this mode, you'll eventually meet two bosses, one for the Heavyweight category and one for the Cruiserweight category. Once you've beaten them, they'll be available as selectable characters. The characters are as follows:
WWW Super Cruiser – Black Widow
WWW Super Heavy – Joe Bruiser

Nintendo 64 A-Z of Cheats Volume 2

WETRIX

Alternate Floors
Complete the eight single player practice rounds, then go to the options screen and select the 'Floor' option to toggle a new background colour and floor pattern. Groovy.

Alternate Playing Pieces
First of all enable the "Alternate Floors" code by completing all eight lessons in one-player practice mode. Then play each of the games except practice and multiplayer and achieve at least an "OK" rating on all of them. The message "Your skill has been noted" will appear when you've done the last one and the background on the main selection screen will turn green. Next select any game mode apart from practice, highlight the little bubble bloke and press A to change him into a duck. Now when you play you'll have normal, small, triangular, rectangular, and square-shaped uppers and downers (man!)

WORLD CUP '98

Change Scoring Sounds
Tap A, B, C Left, or C Down after scoring for different game sounds.

YOSHI'S STORY

Instant Death
For all you sadists out there – and possibly for those of you who find your Yoshi by some quirk of fate stuck in an impossible-to-escape situation – press and hold the Z, A, B and L buttons together and your Yoshi will expire.

Turok 2 Secrets, Strategies, Solutions
ISBN 1-873650-54-X • RRP £9.95

Essential playing guide to one of the biggest games of all time on the Nintendo 64. Complete walkthrough, guide to enemies and objects, and cheats and codes. In addition, the 200-page book features a bonus solution to the original *Turok* game.

**Available at all good book stores and computer outlets.
Also available direct from Paragon Publishing Ltd!**

ORDER NOW!

By phone on **01202 200200**
(international dial +44 1202 200200)

By fax on **01202 299955**
(international dial +44 1202 299955)

By email at **offers@paragon.co.uk**

Nintendo 64 A-Z of Cheats Volume 2

Nintendo 64 Secrets, Strategies, Solutions volume 2
ISBN 1-873650-27-2 • RRP £9.95

The biggest ever collection of Nintendo 64 hints, tips, playing guides and cheats. Superbly illustrated with over 2,000 screen shots and maps. And all in full colour! Includes massive guides for *Bomberman, Duke Nukem, Diddy Kong Racing, Mortal Kombat Trilogy, FIFA '98, Wave Race, Top Gear Rally* and many more! Plus complete A-Z of Nintendo 64 cheats and codes.

**Available at all good book stores and computer outlets.
Also available direct from Paragon Publishing Ltd!**

ORDER NOW!

By phone on **01202 200200**
(international dial +44 1202 200200)

By fax on **01202 299955**
(international dial +44 1202 299955)

By email at **offers@paragon.co.uk**

Zelda 64 Secrets, Strategies, Solutions
ISBN 1-873650-52-3 • RRP £9.95

Exhaustive playing guide to what promises to be the best ever game for Nintendo 64, *Zelda 64*. Includes level guides, character profiles, hidden stages, cheats, tricks and tactics.

**Available at all good book stores and computer outlets.
Also available direct from Paragon Publishing Ltd!**

ORDER NOW!

By phone on **01202 200200**
(international dial +44 1202 200200)

By fax on **01202 299955**
(international dial +44 1202 299955)

By email at **offers@paragon.co.uk**

Nintendo 64 A-Z of Cheats Volume 2

World Cup '98 Secrets, Strategies, Solutions
ISBN 1-873650-37-X • RRP £9.95

A complete guide to scoring, team tactics and player selection for World Cup'98 plus cheats, codes, tricks and techniques for every top Nintendo 64 football game, including *FIFA 64, FIFA: Road to World Cup, International Superstar Soccer* and *J-League Perfect Striker*. An absolute must.

Available at all good book stores and computer outlets.
Also available direct from Paragon Publishing Ltd!

ORDER NOW!

By phone on **01202 200200**
(international dial +44 1202 200200)

By fax on **01202 299955**
(international dial +44 1202 299955)

By email at **offers@paragon.co.uk**

THANK YOU FOR PURCHASING A-Z OF NINTENDO SECRETS, STRATEGIES, SOLUTIONS. VOL 2

Other excellent strategy books in the series include:

Final Fantasy VII Secrets, Strategies, Solutions • £9.95 • ISBN 1 873650 12 4
Gran Turismo Secrets, Strategies, Solutions • £9.95 • ISBN 1 873650 34 5
World Cup '98 Secrets, Strategies, Solutions • £9.95 • ISBN 1 873650 37 X
Tomb Raider II Secrets, Strategies, Solutions • £9.95 • ISBN 1 873650 13 2
Goldeneye Secrets, Strategies, Solutions • £9.95 • ISBN 1 873650 11 6
Lylat Wars Secrets, Strategies, Solutions • £9.95 • ISBN 1 873650 14 0
Mario 64 Secrets, Strategies, Solutions • £9.95 • ISBN 1 873650 07 8
PC Games Vol 1 Secrets, Strategies, Solutions • £9.95 • ISBN 1 873650 18 3
Pocket Book of PC Games Vol 2 SSS • £9.95 • ISBN 1 873650 23 X
A-Z of PlayStation Vol 1 Secrets, Strategies, Solutions • £9.95 • ISBN 1 873650 19 1
A-Z of PlayStation Vol 2 Secrets, Strategies, Solutions • £9.95 • ISBN 1 873650 24 8
A-Z of N64 Vol 1 Secrets, Strategies, Solutions • £9.95 • ISBN 1 873650 25 6
Nintendo 64 Vol 1Secrets, Strategies, Solutions • £14.95 • ISBN 1 873650 08 6
PlayStation Secrets, Strategies, Solutions Vol 1 • £14.95 • ISBN 1 873650 05 1
PlayStation Secrets, Strategies, Solutions Vol 2 • £14.95 • ISBN 1 873650 06 X
PlayStation Secrets, Strategies, Solutions Vol 3 • £14.95 • ISBN 1 873650 15 9

And coming soon...

Zelda 64 Secrets, Strategies, Solutions
Pocket Book of PC Games Vol 3 Secrets, Strategies, Solutions
Tekken 3 Nintendo 64 Secrets, Strategies, Solutions
PlayStation Secrets, Strategies, Solutions Vol 5
Nintendo 64 Secrets, Strategies, Solutions Vol 3
Turok 2 Secrets, Strategies, Solutions